Lovett's Lights on
the Sermon on the mount
matthew 5,6,7

ABOUT THE AUTHOR...DR. C. S. LOVETT

Dr. Lovett is the president of **Personal Christianity Chapel,** a fundamental, evangelical interdenominational ministry. For the past 34 years he has had but one objective — **preparing Christians for the second coming of Christ!** This book is one of over 40 of his works designed to help believers **prepare for His appearing.**

Dr. Lovett's decision to serve the Lord resulted in the loss of a sizable personal fortune. He is well equipped for the job the Lord has given him. A graduate of American Baptist Seminary of the West, he holds the M.A. and M.Div. degrees conferred *Magna Cum Laude.* He has also completed graduate work in psychology at Los Angeles State College and holds an honorary doctorate from the Protestant Episcopal University in London.

A retired Air Force Chaplain (Lt. Colonel), he has been married to Marjorie for over 42 years and has two grown daughters dedicated to the Lord.

Lovett's Lights on
The Sermon on the Mount
matthew 5,6,7

WITH REPHRASED TEXT BY
C.S. Lovett

M.A., M. Div., D.D.

President of Personal Christianity Chapel

Author of fifteen best-selling books including:
Latest Word on The Last Days
Dealing with The Devil
Soul-Winning Made Easy
"Help Lord — The Devil Wants Me Fat!"

Published by
PERSONAL CHRISTIANITY
Baldwin Park, California 91706
1985 Edition
ISBN 0-938148-40-0

© C. S. Lovett 1985

No part of this book may be used or reproduced in any manner whatsoever without written permission of the copyright owner except in articles and reviews.

PRINTED IN THE UNITED STATES OF AMERICA

PREFACE

"Brother Lovett, we've got new translations coming out of our ears today. Do you honestly think we need another one?"

That's the way a Christian brother responded when he first heard about **Lovett's Lights on the New Testament.** As yet he hadn't read any of them, he was simply reacting to the rash of new versions which have appeared in recent years. He thought we were simply coming out with another version. So I took a moment to explain just how **"Lovett's Lights"** bring out the treasures a person usually misses in his private Bible study.

1. Rephrased text. "Lovett's Lights" is NOT a translation. It is a paraphrase. Where two or three words are needed to bring forward the meaning from the original language, you are at liberty to insert them in a paraphrase. You cannot do this in a strict translation. When translators are limited to finding English equivalents for the Greek words, there is often NO WAY to set forth what the Holy Spirit is trying to say. But in a paraphrase there is no such limitation. You can use as many words as you need to make the meaning clear.

2. The Lights. After every few verses you will come upon a paragraph set in different type face and on a shorter line. You will see at once that it is different from the paraphrased text of the Scriptures. These are the **"Lovett's Lights."** Their purpose is to state in as few words as possible the hidden meanings and show how they relate to other great truths of the Bible. Background information such as customs of the times and the way certain words were used in Bible times, are included where they provide the key to interpretation.

3. The Questions. Each author in the New Testament has a definite burden which he tries to communicate in his book. Therefore you will find **key questions** scattered strategically throughout the text to help you keep the writer's burden in view. That way you can evaluate what you are reading in the light of what the author is trying to communicate.

When you put these three things together, you have to agree that **"Lovett's Lights"** does for the reader what no modern version can do. No matter how up-to-date a translation is, it says essentially the same thing as all the other versions. Inasmuch as they DO NOT offer any help with the passages, there is no way for them to expose the deeper meanings of the verses. For the person who does not have the time it takes to DIG into the Word, this is a fantastic blessing.

This is why **"Lovett's Lights on The Sermon on The Mount"** is in your hands. These treasures must be made available to God's people. The average Christian doesn't have the time it takes for the kind of study needed to extract the hidden gems in these passages. Yet they are indispensable. Dear reader, God's Word has the power to change your life. But it can't be done with SURFACE truths. It takes the DEEP truths. And that's what this book gives you. It brings out the buried truths and puts them at your finger tips. When those truths grip you, watch your life change.

Shortly after you begin reading this book of **"Lovett's Lights,"** you will develop a "feel" for what God is saying. Before long you'll be sharing the burden of the apostle and the book will take on a new character. When you see the wealth of biblical understanding that has been opened to you, you won't be able to keep it to yourself.

If you are a Sunday school teacher, it will be natural for you to want to share all this with your students. If you're not a teacher, you may wish to open your home for a Bible study group. You don't have to be a trained teacher to do this. All you have to do is open the book and start using the **"LIGHTS"** as your teaching guide. It will be a lot of fun for you, and exciting for your students. Their eyes will be as wide as owl's as they hear one deep truth after another from your lips. Why some of those lights have enough in them to keep a discussion going for a whole evening.

So don't be afraid to start. The Holy Spirit will back you and make you an exciting teacher the moment you begin sharing these ideas from His Word.

C. S. L.

WELCOME TO THE SCHOOL OF KINGS!

Remember when Prince Charles of England visited the United States before his marriage to Princess Diana? I was jealous of him; not because honors were heaped on him as he toured the nation, but because he could go to one of our Air Force Bases, climb into a jet fighter and take off!

"Oh, wow Margie! Wouldn't it be fabulous to be able to do that!" I was calling to my wife as I stared into the television set. "It sure must be nice to be a prince and enjoy privileges like that. How I'd love to fly one of those new fighters!"

"Honey, she said, "You're drooling aren't you?"

INTRO a

I guess I was. As a WWII Pilot, I'd flown all kinds of propeller driven aircraft, but never a jet. I've looked at those sleek, modern fighters and longed to get in one and slice up the sky.

"You're right dear, I'm not only drooling, I'm dreaming." Then I sighed, "It sure must be nice."

THEN CAME THE OTHER SIDE

There are always two sides to every story — even Charles'. When he was interviewed on TV later that day, we got the other side. The life of a prince really isn't as rosy as it appears. For Charles went on to speak rather bitterly of the rigors he had to endure while being groomed for the throne of England.

"Growing up as a prince," he complained, "is almost like being a slave." I began to feel sorry for him as he described all he had to go through. He had to become fluent in a number of languages and be familiar with the arts and sciences. It seems a prince of England is expected to know everything. He had to master history and was tutored for hours at a time in finance and statesmanship. Day after day he was schooled in heraldry and diplomacy. It was essential that he become expert in protocol.

Having endured such constant schooling, Charles moaned, "I practically had no life of my own. I was like a servant under the authority of others all the time." Even now when he is married, he's still not his own man. A great deal is expected of both him and Di. The truth is, he's still in the SCHOOL OF KINGS. He's still being groomed for the throne.

WE'RE IN THE SAME BOAT

No, we're not being groomed to reign over England

we're being groomed to reign with Christ (Rev. 5:10). As Paul Billheimer put it in his popular book, we're DESTINED FOR THE THRONE. As sons of God, we're **princes** as surely as Charles. And God is getting us ready to reign in Christ's kindgom — **if we'll let Him.** In our case, we have a choice. We don't have to absorb the schooling if we don't want to. At least, we don't have to pay attention in class.

Our schooling is no easier for us than it is for Charles. In fact, it may even be harder. While Charles labors in the worldly school of languages, science, history, statesmanship, protocol. . . etc., we slug it out in a different classroom.

Even though we're SONS OF GOD, we are put through an earthly life filled with DISAPPOINTMENTS, TRAGEDIES, ABUSES, and the struggle to survive. On top of that, we're surrounded by fraud, corruption, greed, lusts of every kind, polution, both mental and moral. We're taxed and tempted. Sickness can strike at any time. We really don't know what to expect from one day to the next. We live on the edge of uncertainty. Yet, every bit of it is good stuff for transforming us into the likeness of the Lord.

Like Charles, we may groan when we're exploited by others and suffer loss. We may resent the pressures that come through marriage, raising teen-agers, holding down a job, trying to make ends meet, and the fact that they never stop, never let up. But God knows what He's doing. He knows how to run His school. He knows what it takes to get the job done. And it won't do us one bit of good to complain. He knows how He made us and He figures we can take the grooming for the BRIEF TIME we're on earth. A person can take almost anything, if he knows better times are ahead.

INTRO a

YOU KNOW WHAT GOD WANTS, DON'T YOU?

God created us in HIS IMAGE, you know that. But He can't make us LIKE HIMSELF. I mean, He can't create us as FREEWILL creatures and at the same time have his **character** found in us. Even though we're made of the SAME STUFF as God, it's impossible for Him to PUT His CHARACTER into us. So what does He do? He puts us through the SCHOOL OF KINGS. That's what this life is all about. It's a special course for the sons of God. That course consists of the pressures of this life and how we react to them. It is how we react to the situations of life THAT BUILDS OUR CHARACTER.

God's ambition for us is that we'll respond with the RIGHT REACTIONS and in the process BECOME LIKE HIM. However, if we don't want to, that's up to us. God gave us free wills and He won't interfere with our choices. But we need to realize this one life on earth is our SINGLE OPPORTUNITY to become like the Lord. And if we want to REIGN WITH JESUS, we've got to make the most of this opportunity to BECOME LIKE HIM.

The wash out rate is high in the SCHOOL OF KINGS. Many Christians cannot be bothered. They don't care about getting ahead in Christ, they're too busy getting ahead in the world. To them the school means nothing. As a result of their chasing FAME, FAMILY, and FORTUNE, they fail the course and are disqualified. They don't lose their salvation of course. They're still God's SONS and will be with Him in the kingdom, but they will not reign with Him. They will NOT BE KINGS.

Just because a person is DESTINED FOR THE THRONE, doesn't mean he's going to make it. All anyone is guaranteed IS THE OPPORTUNITY to make it. Every single Christian has an EQUAL CHANCE to qualify, but only those who seize the opportunity of this schooling will actually sit on the throne.

NOT A SNAP COURSE

Remember when you were in college, some of the courses were easy. . . snap courses? Along with your heavy subjects, you took some light ones to balance the load. Well, the school of kings has no snap courses. It's tough all the way. Anyone who thinks the Christian life is easy is not really involved in it. I mean, he's not even going to class. He doesn't even know what's going on.

Anyone who tells another, "Come to Jesus and all your troubles will be over," is a deceiver. He may not mean to deceive, but what he's saying is the OPPOSITE of the truth. The truth is, the Christian life is rough. It's not for sissies. Why? Those who set their hearts on being like Christ, who long to please God with their lives — must make awful sacrifices.

The Christian life is SACRIFICE from beginning to end — for those who commit themselves to live for Jesus. It costs a man all he has to go through the school of kings and graduate with honors. It has to become an OBSESSION, so that with Paul he says, "**This one thing I do. . .** " (Phil. 3:13). Inasmuch as Jesus has committed Himself to us 100%. . . He has every right to expect the same from us.

• Have you ever watched salmon on television, fighting swift rivers to reach their spawning grounds? How desperately they attack the falls. They leap furiously and fall back again and again. Yet they don't give up. They'd rather die than not press on.

Those are just fish, with nothing to gain but planting their eggs. How much more desperately should the Christian struggle against this world in trying to please the Lord. His eternal future is at stake. The rewards are beyond anything our minds can conceive.

NOW'S THE TIME TO SACRIFICE

• Here's a young man working his way through medical school. He wants to be a doctor. But it's tough. He has to work to make a living, and at the same time keep up his grades. There are lots of places he can't go, things he has to do without. To get his education he has to burn the midnight oil and sacrifice many good times. Most of the time he feels left out, missing a great deal. But there's no choice — if he wants that career.

Ah, but when he finally graduates and becomes established in his profession, will he regret the sacrifice? No Way. He'll be glad he forfeited the temporary pleasures in order to win the grander prize of a satisfying career.

THE SAME IS TRUE OF US.

We've been invited to EARN a fabulous career with Christ, an ETERNAL CAREER. But we have to go through the school of kings to qualify. While we're in school, we must bear down, sacrifice and work hard. We have to pass up all kinds of things, pleasures and possessions, if we want to keep up our grades. To win the prize, we must graduate. The top jobs of heaven go to the top graduates.

What the Lord asks of us, by way of sacrifice, is to shun the world's offers. He wants us to abandon the struggle to GET AHEAD IN THE WORLD, and take up the struggle to GET AHEAD IN HIM. It's so easy to seek what the world seeks — fame, family, and fortune, but we have to forego that. Yet it's a TEMPORARY SACRIFICE. You and I are on this planet for only a few years. They go by SO FAST. The Lord asks us to TRADE THE TEMPORARY FOR THE ETERNAL. If we make that sacrifice, He guarantees we WON'T BE SORRY.

> "As it is written, eye hath not seen nor ear heard, neither has entered into the heart of man the things that God has prepared for those who love Him." (1 Cor. 2:9)

WHAT MAKES THE SCHOOL SO TOUGH?

"Have you ever read a book on how to grow weeds?"

- I asked that of my congregation one Sunday morning. The audience chuckled. The idea of learning how to grow weeds is ridiculous. Everyone knows you don't have to do anything to grow weeds. Leave the ground alone and you'll get plenty. But if you want a crop, you have to prepare the ground, plant

INTRO a

seed, water and cultivate the soil. Finally it has to be harvested. That's a lot of work.

Then I took a large book and held it up for all to see. Holding it at arm's length, I asked,

"If I want this book to fall to the floor, will I need to do something special? Would I have to give the book instructions on how to fall?"

The audience again chuckled, thinking I was trying to be funny. But I was leading up to something. Then I relaxed my grip on the book and it landed on the floor with a thud.

"What did I have to do to get that book to go down to the floor?"

"NOTHING!" came the response from my people.

"And that is the WAY OF THE WORLD. If you want to BE LIKE THE WORLD, you don't have to do anything. Just drift with the tide. You'll BE LIKE THE WORLD, as easily as weeds growing in an idle field."

THEN I GOT DOWN ON THE FLOOR

I took the book and placed it on my chest. From the prone position, I asked the audience, chuckling even more by now:

"If I want this book to GO UP, how am I going to get it to do that?"

The reply came back, "You have to push it up!"

Ah, they were getting the point. It takes no force to drop anything. But if you want it to go in an upward direction, you have to OVERCOME the force of gravity. The course of this world is like gravity — DOWN.

The hardest thing about space flight is escaping the earth's gravity. You've seen those huge booster rockets burst into flame, engulfing the launch pad in fire and smoke. It takes enormous power to get those shuttle buses off the ground.

INTRO a

The same is true of the Christian life. The way of the Lord is UP. The way of the world is DOWN. To go down, you need only to EXIST. The world will automatically take you down. But to go UP, you have to fight like those salmon to overcome the pull of the world. You have to put forth tremendous effort. Yet overcoming is only HALF THE PROBLEM. For when you start to GO UP, an even bigger problem presents itself. YOU BECOME DIFFERENT FROM THE WORLD.

BECOMING DIFFERENT

• A young girl wants to attend a special event at school, but her parents can't afford a new dress for the occasion. So her mother takes an old dress and

tries to refashion it on her sewing machine. But she's not ready for her daughter's reaction when she sees it. "MOTHER! I'LL JUST DIE IF I HAVE TO WEAR THAT!" She means it, too. More than one girl has made herself sick — just so she could stay home. The saying is true, "People would rather be dead than different!"

Most of us are like that. We want people to think well of us and we're crushed if they don't. Those feelings of rejection can make us sick. This is why Christians do not speak out for Jesus. They're afraid of what people will think of them if they do. This is clearly a Christ-hating world, and when a person is identified with Him, some of that hatred rubs off. One has only to say a little about Jesus to be branded as a fanatic. So here's the big silencer — "WHAT WILL PEOPLE THINK!"

Why do Christians feel they must drive late model cars, wear new clothes and live in the best possible house? They don't want to be out of step with the world. They'd rather conform than be different. Without realizing it, **that attitude locks them into the world.** The same Christians will not admit this,

INTRO a

but what the world thinks is more important to them than what God thinks. Unless a believer does something about that attitude, he probably should forget about the school of kings. He won't like the course. For you see, the CURRICULUM of the school of kings is THE SERMON ON THE MOUNT.

Did you get what I just said: the curriculum or course for the school of kings, is the SERMON ON THE MOUNT. And it's a tough course.

TOUGH COURSE

"BE YE PERFECT, EVEN AS YOUR FATHER IN HEAVEN IS PERFECT."

That's what you're going to run into in the sermon. And if we let it stand as it reads, or as it strikes your spirit when you see those words, then I ask, "Can you do that? Can you **be** that? Can your whole life measure up to such a perfect standard?"

No way. No one other than Jesus has come close to the perfect standard. Even the apostle Paul insisted he hadn't arrived, though he was determined to TRY. And God, being God, cannot set LESS than a perfect standard. So what do we do? Are we condemned to failure before we start? If that's what it takes to graduate from the school of kings, who can make it?

Relax, it's not as bad as it sounds. God knows we cannot measure up to a PERFECT STANDARD. The flesh is too powerful. Besides, it has too big a head start. This is why Jesus said, "The spirit is willing, but the flesh is weak" (Matt. 26:41). Some might think having the HOLY SPIRIT guarantees perfect lives, but it doesn't. What it guarantees IS A WAR — a war between the flesh and the spirit. The apostle Paul put it this way:

INTRO a

"For the flesh lusteth against the Spirit and the Spirit against the flesh: and these are CONTRARY the one to the other: so that ye CANNOT do the things that ye would" (Gal. 5:17).

See the word "CANNOT?" Paul was speaking to Christians, explaining the real struggle of the Christian life. That word "cannot" should not be tampered with, for it's the awesome truth. When the apostle Paul had resolved this matter in his own mind, he said:

"So then I find this law at work: When I want to do good, evil is right there with me. For in my inner being (new nature) I delight in God's Law, but I see another law at work in the members of my body, waging WAR against the law of my mind... so then, I myself in my mind am a slave to God's law, but in the sinful nature a slave to sin" (Rom 7:21-23, 25 NIV).

Do you see the WAR? You're in the midst of it. And when you try to live godly, you'll find how much of a fight it is.

Above I said relax. God knows we cannot measure up to the perfect standard. So now I am going to share with you one of Scripture's SUPER SECRETS. Even though we can never attain to the perfection set forth in God's standard — WE CAN TRY. And here's the secret:

With God: Trying Is Winning!

WHY THE STANDARD, THEN?

Why would God set forth a perfect standard if He knows we cannot reach it? Why make the curriculum of the school of kings something beyond

INTRO a

us? The answer is simple. God must have some standard by which to measure us. If He didn't use His own CHARACTER as the standard of measurement, who's would He use? Since there is no other for Him to use, He's going to measure us by HIMSELF. And why not? The reason we're on this earth is to become like Him (Rom. 8:29). So if there is going to be a standard of GOD-LIKENESS, what better than God's own character.

So that's what we find in the sermon on the mount — the perfect standard. That's why it is the curriculum of the school of kings. This is what God asks us to strive for, even though He knows we'll never make it as long as we're in these bodies. At the same time it gives Him a perfect device for measuring our efforts and progress.

The harder we try to be like Him, the more He's pleased with us. And when we're willing to turn our backs on the world to do this, He is gaining for Himself the kind of people with whom He wants to spend eternity.

WHY THE SCHOOL IS NEEDED

The Lord Jesus has a problem. He's going to INHERIT the world, and He will have the task of running it. Now that is an awesome job when you consider the problems rulers and presidents have running their governments. In the United States, for example, one out of every five workers is employed by the government. It takes a lot of people to keep this country going. Think how many it will take to run the world.

That's the Lord's problem. Where is He going to get the people to work with Him in His administration? There will be jobs ranging from cabinet offices, those who work the closest to Him, ambassadorships, department and agency heads, as well as those who sit on commissions and fill advisory posts. In the U.S. there are more than 40,000 such jobs and our presidents have an awful time finding the right people.

INTRO a

Then there are those who sweep out the government buildings, scour latrines and work in the dumps. That also will be true of Jesus' administration. There will be HIGH POSTS and menial jobs. He'll have no trouble getting people to clean the streets and empty trash, but where will He get those who'll reign with Him, who'll run the government with Him?

AH. . . from the school of kings. Those who complete the course, giving it their best effort, will get those jobs. They'll be the cream of the crop.

INTRO a

22

Why? They will have sacrificed the world and all it offers, to put Jesus first. They will have worked hard to please Him. They have sacrificed THE PRESENT to win THE FUTURE. They believe Jesus when He says, "You won't be sorry" (Matt. 19:29). So they burn the midnight oil, deny themselves in order to make good grades. They want to make sure TOP JOBS await them when they graduate.*

---

*Did you know GREAT DIFFERENCES will exist between Christians in heaven, differences in RANK and CLOSENESS TO JESUS? If you're interested in the Scriptural basis for this truth, you'll appreciate the author's book. . . IT'S YOUR TURN TO BE BLESSED. There, the whole matter of our future jobs with Jesus is laid out as well as its Scriptural background.

THE OPPORTUNITY OF A LIFETIME

Now that you know about the school of kings and why it is needed, you have come upon the opportunity of a lifetime. I'm pretty sure you didn't know thousands of HIGH POSTS are waiting to be filled and that you have a clear field when it comes to securing one for yourself. You don't hear much about this. It isn't preached. In American Christianity, the big emphasis is "Get 'em saved." Little happens after that. You're not challenged to compete for an exalted position in eternity. And yet, it's easily within your power to win one of the highest jobs in heaven — FOREVER!

If you think you'd like a SUPER JOB with Jesus, then get serious about the school of kings. Be ready to sacrifice worldly pleasures and comforts, or even suffer scorn for Christ and I guarantee you, there is no way to miss. You'll be alongside the Lord, with your RANK blazing from your forehead.

And here's why I can be so definite about that guarantee. Very few Christians know about these jobs, consequently very few are going after them. The field is wide open. What's more, very few Christians CARE ANYTHING about life with Jesus in the kingdom. They're too involved with this world. That leaves it all for you. So go for it. Anyone can make it: man, woman, talented, untalented, it makes no difference. For once again, to win with God, all you have to do is TRY. It's the opportunity of a lifetime!

THIS TRUTH DEMONSTRATED

As I was working on this page, President Reagan paid a special visit to the campus of Washington College. He went there to honor a Vietnamese boy

INTRO a

who was graduating with honors. He had made straight "A"s and was the valedictorian of the class.

Now that is astonishing when you consider he couldn't speak a word of English when he started. You see, this boy had escaped from the Communists in Viet Nam by putting to sea in an open boat. He was one of the few boat people that made it to land and thence to the United States. When he enrolled in the school, he sacrificed everything and worked desperately to learn. And now here he was, the top student in his class. So outstanding was he, he was awarded a scholarship to M.I.T.

To the Vietnamese, and others like them, America offers a FABULOUS OPPORTUNITY. A free education is available. And do they work to take advantage of it. They'll forgo everything just to

get that education, because they know that with it, THE SKY IS THE LIMIT. What a contrast to our American youth who do all they can to avoid an education.

I think you see the application.

God has established this life as the school of kings. The amazing opportunity of a TOP JOB with Jesus beckons. That job is ETERNAL, nothing like the temporary honors and pleasures of this world. But Christians have to **seize** the opportunity. They have to get in and study, work hard, burn the midnight oil, avoid anything that would deter them, sacrifice everything if necessary, to graduate with honors.

As we come to the SERMON ON THE MOUNT, you'll learn what is expected of you. You'll see what it takes to please God, what it takes to BE LIKE HIM. I know it will be rough, but it'll be worth it. You can be sure Charles will be quite happy once he's seated on the throne of England. And you'll be very happy to have your job close to Christ. You won't regret your sacrifices then. Now that you have an idea of what is coming as you read this book, let me welcome you. . .

TO THE SCHOOL OF KINGS!

BEFORE YOU READ THE SERMON ON THE MOUNT

• One night after prayer meeting, my friend Frank Hutchinson approached me:

"Can I ask you a question?"

"Sure."

"I've been thinking a lot lately about pleasing the Lord. Do you know of any book or material written specifically to tell a person how to please God? I mean, that gives the steps... 1—2—3 — like your books do?"

"Yes, there's a fabulous work on that. It's called the Sermon on the Mount."

NOT WHAT HE WANTED

"Oh, I wasn't thinking of a sermon. I meant a practical book."

Frank was no different from most in his view of the Sermon on the Mount. It's the title that does it. It creates the wrong impression in people's minds. They see Jesus standing on the side of a mountain preaching A SERMON — one among many. So to most, **it's just another sermon.**

But it's not that at all. It might better be called, **HOW TO LIVE A GOD-PLEASING LIFE.** It is a course, actually — one which has 8 steps. If you chose to call it EIGHT STEPS TO A GOD-PLEASING LIFE, you'd be right on target. So I assured Frank if he took a hard look at "THE SERMON," he'd not be disappointed. He'd find exactly what he was looking for. Then I added:

INTRO B

"At the same time, Frank, there are some things you should know about THE SERMON before you start reading it. There are things that SHOULD BE IN YOUR MIND — otherwise what you read will raise questions you can't answer — and that will perplex you. This can be a most perplexing formula — if you don't know what's going on. So let me mention some things everyone should know BEFORE reading the sermon."

FIRST — ABOUT THE BEATITUDES

You know what those are — that list of EIGHT BLESSEDS you encounter right off the bat. Someone has called them "BE-attitudes." By that is meant, those 8 Blesseds make up the attitudes we should have toward God and our fellow man in the circumstances that confront us daily. These attitudes should be installed in our being, hence BE-attitudes.

But here's what's often missed. The 8 Beatitudes are **the foundation** for the rest of the sermon. The entire sermon, as you know, covers three chapters of Matthew's gospel, 5-6-7. But the Beatitudes consist of only EIGHT VERSES. How can they be the foundation? Ah — the Beatitudes describe THE CHARACTER of the man who pleases God. They show what is expected of those growing up in the school of kings.

Look closely at the Beatitudes and you'll see all 8 have to do with CHARACTER. What then is the rest of the sermon for? If what is expected of us is found in those eight verses, why does the Lord go on for 3 chapters? This is what I wanted Frank to see. So that His listeners would not misunderstand what He means by the Beatitudes, the Lord went on to show how a man of this **character WOULD ACT** in specific situations. In other words, the CONDUCT of a man with this kind of character.

INTRO B

Jesus knew that simply reciting the Beatitudes wouldn't do the job. The people couldn't possibly make the applicaiton for themselves. So He went on to mention any number of situations that might confront a Christian and then described the God-pleaser's CONDUCT in those situations. That's what the Sermon on the Mount is all about.

If you were to skim through the 3 chapters after reading the Beatitudes, you'd find Him describing all sorts of situations, such as PRAYING, GIVING, WORRYING, FASTING, JUDGING OTHERS, MAKING OATHS, ACCUMULATING WEALTH, ETC. What you'd be reading would be the BEATITUDE CHARACTER in action. Graphically it looks like this:

BEATITUDES

Character

Blessed are . . .

1. the poor in spirit
2. those who mourn
3. the meek
4. those who hunger for righteousness
5. the merciful
6. the pure in heart
7. the peacemakers
8. the persecuted

REST OF THE SERMON

INTRO B

Conduct (Character in Action in Situations)

murder
adultery
divorce
loving enemies
retaliation
giving
prayer
worry
fasting
judging others
treasures in heaven
making oaths
seeking, knocking
false/true teachers
two ways to go
keeping the Law
being reconciled
salt and light

29

But there's more to see.

Observe the 8 Beatitudes above. The first 4 are TOWARD GOD. The next four have to do WITH

INTRO B

OTHERS. Thus the first four are VERTICAL, the next four are HORIZONTAL. The division is like this:

Character	
TOWARD GOD	the poor in spirit* those who mourn the meek those who hunger for righteousness
TOWARD OTHERS	the merciful the pure in heart the peacemakers the persecuted*

*"Theirs is the kingdom of heaven."

OBSERVATION

Note how the first one ("Poor in spirit") and the last one ("The persecuted") have the SAME COMPENSATION. Both are said to **"receive the kingdom of heaven."** How come? Well, being POOR IN SPIRIT is the beginning point of the Christian life, hence it is also the beginning point of the school of kings. A believer must be poor in spirit, even to be saved. Yet once he is saved, he is immediately involved in the school of kings. When Jesus says the kingdom of heaven belongs to the beginner, who is poor in spirit, it means this Christian is immediately locked into the heavenly family. All the opportunities of being a PRINCE are before him. He can now start working his way up the BEATITUDE-LADDER, which is the course or curriculum of the school of kings.

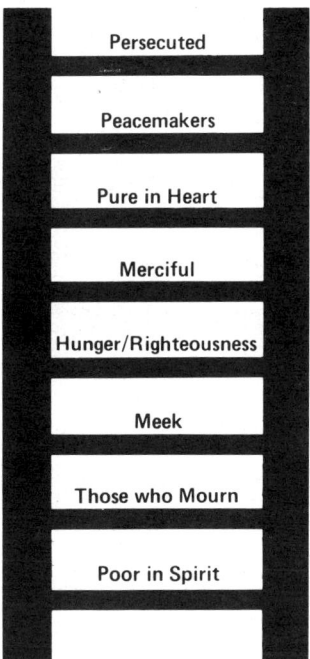

BEATITUDE LADDER

- Persecuted
- Peacemakers
- Pure in Heart
- Merciful
- Hunger/Righteousness
- Meek
- Those who Mourn
- Poor in Spirit

By taking the 8 steps of the Beatitudes and putting the POOR IN SPIRIT at the bottom, we create the BEATITUDE LADDER. In this ascending order we see that the curriculum of the school of kings is quite a climb. This is the right way to look at the Beatitudes, for it is definitely an upward road. Those making it to the top have come quite a distance. They've made a lot of changes into the likeness of the Lord.

INTRO B

When Jesus says those who are persecuted for righteousness sake also receive the kingdom of heaven, He is referring to the man who has climbed the EIGHT STEPS of the Beatitude ladder and is groomed for his future job in the kingdom. He is ready to graduate. He has it made, so to speak. Thus the kingdom is his.

In the case of the one who is "poor in spirit," he has his future job **potentially.** In the case of the latter, the "persecuted" man, he **actually** has it made, having completed the course. Both are IN the kingdom, but the one who graduates with honors, is the one who truly has it made.

A final thing about the Beatitudes: after you complete the course and become a God-pleaser, here's what you can expect:

> **"Blessed are you when people insult you, persecute you and falsely say all kinds of evil against you because of Me."** (Vs. 11)

Isn't that something! As someone who has struggled against the world, like salmon fighting the falls, what do you get for your trouble? Persecution! But that persecution comes from the world. That is to be expected, since this world hates Christ. Having succeeded in acquiring the BE-attitudes of Christ, you're going to be like Him. If this world hates Him, it will not like you. However, by that time, you will have ceased to worry about what the world thinks. Your heart will be fixed on what Jesus thinks:

> **"Rejoice and be glad, for GREAT is your reward in heaven!"**

Therefore don't let the threat of persecution

dampen your zeal. You're only going to be in this world for a short time anyway. Then you'll be meeting Jesus in the sky. In that moment, you'll be glad you suffered for Him. You'll never regret having suffered abuse or scorn for His sake when you're looking into His eyes. Your reward will be so fantastic, God can't even tell us what it is — now.

THE SECOND THING YOU SHOULD KNOW

I've just mentioned persecution. There are Christians who can't bear that idea, even though the Lord said it was part of the package. Neither do these people believe it is necessary for anyone to TRY to acquire the God-pleasing CHARACTER of the Beatitudes. "Impossible!" they say. "Impractical! It does not make sense for today!" So what do they do? THEY TRY TO GET RID OF THE SERMON. The most popular method for sidestepping the Sermon is to say: "It doesn't belong to our time."

INTRO B

Inasmuch as Jesus frequently refers to the "kingdom of heaven," some nervous Christians seize upon that and insist the SERMON belongs to a future time. It applies, they say, to the time when Christ's kingdom is on earth, THE MILLENNIUM. "People will be able to live it then," they offer. So they teach other Christians to FORGET the Sermon on the Mount for now.

But when you read it for yourself and find Jesus with His disciples gathered about Him, you see He's clearly telling them **what they're to be like in the world** after He's gone. Were you to turn to Romans 12 and read verses 14-21, you'd think you were reading the Sermon on the Mount. It's like that through all of Paul's letters. Whenever he speaks of tenderheartedness and forgiveness, his words are rooted in the Sermon. If the Sermon on the Mount is not for today, then neither are Paul's letters.

Why do I mention this? Should you get involved in the Sermon and GET EXCITED about the God-pleasing life, some well meaning Christian might try to throw cold water on your ambition. Should he tell you the Sermon is not for today, tell him to bug off, because everything the New Testament has to say about loving each other and forgiving each other is rooted in Jesus' words in the Sermon.

> **NOTE.** Matthew has collected in Chapters 5-6-7 the heart of what Jesus taught as He went through the towns and villages of Israel during His earthly ministry. Under the inspiration of the Holy Spirit, Matthew put them together in such a way, we get the connection between the Beatitudes and the illustrations that follow them. This is God's way of providing for us a clear view of what's required of us in the school of kings. Jesus taught these same things everywhere He went. You find these truths scattered through the other gospels. For example see Luke 11:33-36; 12:22-24; 13:24.

THE THIRD THING YOU NEED TO KNOW

The reason some declare the Sermon "impossible" and "impractical" is because they don't recognize TO WHOM it is directed. Let me say flatly it is addressed to the NEW MAN **and to him alone.** No one but the NEW MAN could begin to do any of these things, nor want to.

What do I mean by the NEW MAN?

With your Bible open to Genesis 2:7, you'll read that God "FORMED" man out of the dust. That gives him a body. I'll draw that, like this:

BODY

Then you'll read, God breathed into him the "BREATH OF LIFE." That gives him his spirit.

SPIRIT / BODY

And then he became a "LIVING SOUL."

SOUL / SPIRIT / BODY

Thus we have a complete man: BODY — SPIRIT — SOUL. When this man comes to Jesus he receives the SPIRIT OF CHRIST. Now he has 2 spirits.

INTRO B

What does that do to our drawing? Ah, the spirit of man has to move over to make room for the Spirit of Christ. So now our man looks like this:

See how the same soul now has TWO SPIRITS - the spirit of man and the Spirit of Christ. The body, soul, and Spirit of Christ constitute the "new creation." It is as though the "old man" has moved over to make room for the "new man," so that the two dwell side by side in the one body.

Look what we have here. We have TWO PEOPLE (in a sense) living in one body. We have a body, soul, and spirit of man, making a complete man. The Bible calls him the OLD MAN. We also have the same body, the same soul and the Spirit of Christ, which makes up another man — the NEW MAN. Since this really is a new man, the Bible also refers to him as a "new creation" (2 Cor. 5:17). The Bible also refers to these two men by other names. The OLD MAN is spoken of as "THE FLESH" and the NEW MAN is referred to as "THE SPIRIT." For our purposes, we'll remember the **old man** as a BRUTE and the **new man** as a BABY.

THE OLD NATURE IS A BULLY

When a man is saved, his new nature is a helpless infant. Perfect, but still a baby. Some Christians grow very fast, others grow little in an entire lifetime. As the new man grows, the believer gets stronger and stronger. He finds the bully winning fewer and fewer battles. In time, the tables turn and the believer's victories outnumber his defeats. At first, a true Christian is shocked by the amount of sin in his life. He hates it. If he means business for Jesus, he'll dedicate himself to putting muscle on that new man as fast as he can.

IT'S THE NEW MAN WE CARE ABOUT

We don't have to instruct the OLD MAN, he already knows the ways of the world. We don't have to teach him how to be bad. He's headed DOWN and would drag us (the soul) with him if he could. It's the NEW MAN we're concerned with. This new creation needs help — lots of it. He's a baby involved in an UPHILL FIGHT. He's like that salmon trying to leap those falls and get upstream.

Where does this baby get help and instruction for living a godly life? The world won't help him, it doesn't know how. It would only make him like itself — evil. Only the Bible has this kind of infor-

INTRO B

mation. And if he wants SPECIFIC INSTRUCTIONS as to how to please the Lord, the SERMON provides the particulars. But if the new man is neglected; if nothing is done to direct him and he is left to himself, he will go the way of the world. The Christian life is a WARFARE, one which cannot be won WITHOUT A FIGHT (Gal. 5:17). so it's urgent that the NEW MAN be schooled in the Sermon on the Mount. That alone will show him what's expected of him, what he's to be like.

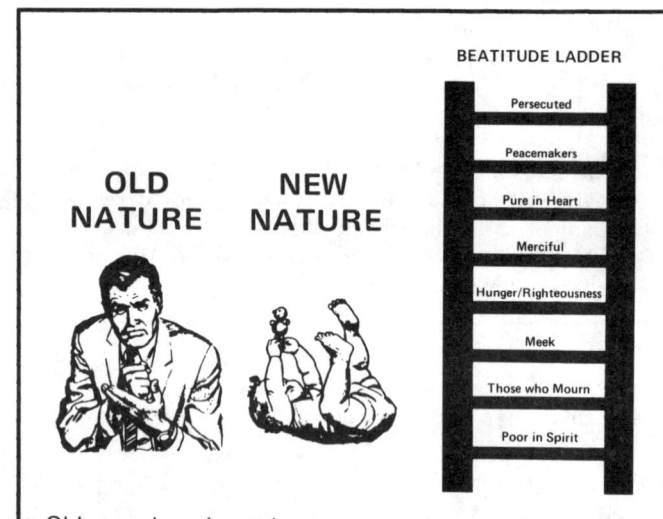

OLD NATURE   **NEW NATURE**

BEATITUDE LADDER
- Persecuted
- Peacemakers
- Pure in Heart
- Merciful
- Hunger/Righteousness
- Meek
- Those who Mourn
- Poor in Spirit

Old man doesn't need a sermon on how to be bad. But new man craves to be like God, because the Spirit he has received hungers for righteousness.

THE FOURTH THING ONE SHOULD KNOW

Remember the TV show, "NAME THAT TUNE?" Different contestants would try to guess the name of a song simply by hearing 5 or 6 notes. Well, I did something like that with my congregation to demonstrate the FOURTH THING a person should know before reading the Sermon on the Mount.

I went to the piano and struck the B-flat key three times.

"Anyone know what song I have in mind?"

Understandably, there was no answer. They didn't have enough to work with. That was my point. For you see, the SAME THING IS TRUE when it comes to handling specific Bible passages. As you know, many will turn to a particular verse and try to figure out what it means just by looking at the words. They can't do it, of course. If they try, they're almost certain to get error.

It's a basic rule of Bible handling that you have to have the WHOLE PICTURE before you can grasp the parts. You have to know the CONTEXT of what the Lord is saying before you can rightly handle a specific statement. Much error abounds in the church today because many come to certain passages in just this way. People will turn to a little verse and try to figure what it means without first grasping the whole chapter or learning what that particular book of the Bible is all about.

• A friend in the East calls me regularly, often with questions about specific Bible passages. He'll say for example, "Dr. Lovett when Jesus says, 'Blessed are the meek,' what does He mean?" See — he picks a specific verse and wants me to give a one sentence answer. Knowing I couldn't, I'd reply:

"Larry, before I can explain what that verse means, I have to tell you what's going on here, what the Lord is trying to do, what He's trying to get across to His disciples."

INTRO B

When there is time, I give Larry the overall picture and then show how the specific verse fits into it. Then he says, "Oh, I see." He does see, for when you have the whole picture, the answer is usually obvious. If a person reads the admonition to give his jacket to the someone who wants his shirt and he blindly tries to follow the **surface meaning** of the verse, he'd soon be out of clothes. Or food or money or whatever any street-bum might ask. So the true meaning has to involve more than is seen on the surface of the verse.

Don't try to figure out what the Lord is saying in some of the specific verses of the Sermon until you learn what the Sermon itself is all about. You'll end up with error if you do.

HERE'S THE LAST THING YOU SHOULD KNOW

You've seen M.A.S.H. on TV, — the hospital comedy series set in the Korean conflict. You've watched Hawkeye and BJ and Radar and Klinger. I'm sure you've noticed the chaplain on the show, Father Mulkahy. He's a regular guy. I mean he smokes and drinks with the fellows, even gambles with them. He's one of them and it makes him popular. No doubt he feels he's a real encouragement to them, joining in at their level.

But did you ever see anyone come to him for spiritual help?

He can't minister to anyone, because he's one of them.

Why do I tell that? If you take the Sermon on the Mount seriously and start TRYING to display the character revealed in the Beatitudes, you'll gradually become different from those around you. This will separate you from them and that can be rough. People don't mix with those who are different. You need to face this possible rejection, for it can be painful. Here's what you have to think about — Do I want to please God or those around me? If you set your heart to please God, you will be different.

But that's where your power lies.

The gospel has the power to CHANGE PEOPLE. Its power is seen when it makes us different from those of the world. The shame of the modern church is that you can scarcely tell the difference between Christians and non-Christians. They look the same, talk and think the same, even do business the same way. Yet, it's only when WE'RE DIFFERENT that we display the life-changing power of the gospel. Only when we display that difference will people come to us for spiritual help. It's the difference that ATTRACTS them. "I don't know what it is about you," they'll say, "but something makes me feel you're a person I can talk to, someone who might have the answer."

WHAT YOU'VE LEARNED

Not only have you learned about the SCHOOL OF KINGS, you've also learned FIVE THINGS that should be in your mind before you read the Sermon. Now you're prepared for it.

Here are the five things again:

1. The 8 Beatitudes are the FOUNDATION for the rest of the Sermon. They set forth the CHARACTER it takes to please God. The rest of the SERMON shows how a person WITH THAT CHARACTER acts in specific situations.

INTRO B

INTRO B

2. The Sermon on the Mount is for today, regardless what anyone tells you — even if the notes of the Scofield Bible say otherwise.

3. The sermon is addressed to your NEW MAN only. Godly living is a spiritual matter — something your FLESH (old man) despises. The conflict between your OLD MAN (flesh/brute) and your NEW MAN (spirit/baby) is what makes living the Sermon on the Mount an uphill fight.

4. Don't try to handle individual passages of the SERMON until you have a grasp of the whole picture. Once you know what the Lord is really after, it is easy to interpret His words in particular verses. Trying to deal with specific passages without this grasp could lead you into error.

5. When you begin to LIVE the Sermon, changes will occur in you that will make you DIFFERENT from those around you. But that difference is glorious. It is proof you're successfully climbing the Beatitude-ladder. It assures your graduation from the SCHOOL OF KINGS. If your difference brings the scorn of those around you, just remember Jesus' words, "DO NOT BE LIKE THEM."

Finally, if the task of living the Sermon on the Mount seems impossible at any point, remember that with God . . .

TRYING IS WINNING!

matt. 5

43

As Jesus traveled throughout Galilee, He healed vast numbers of people of all kinds of diseases, even the paralytic, epileptic and demon-possessed. As a result, His fame spread far and wide. Large crowds began to follow Him, coming from one end of Israel to the other. The sermon on the mount was preached on one of those occasions when masses of people were closing in on Him and His disciples.

matt. 5

**THE BEATITUDES
THE COURSE FOR THE SCHOOL OF KINGS
(The character of the God-pleaser)**

1. So when Jesus saw the crowds, He went up on the side of a mountain and sat down. And when His disciples had gathered around Him, 2. He began to speak out, teaching them:

3. Blessed are those who realize they're poor in spirit,
 for theirs is the kingdom of heaven.

BLESSED. The wind carried Jesus' first word to their ears and what a sweet sounding word — "BLESSED." That's what the crowd had come for . . . blessing. This word has to do with HAPPINESS, but a different kind of happiness from that which the world seeks. The world you see, has its kind of happiness and God has His. Men think they're happy when their outward CIRCUMSTANCES are the way they like them, when they can do what they want. But that kind of happiness is based on the UPS & DOWNS of life. It comes and goes. Jesus is referring to TRUE HAPPINESS, permanent happiness, which is NOT BASED ON EXTERNALS, but flows from a man's CHARACTER. It is INTERNAL, the by-product of what a MAN IS, not what he has. Things can go wrong outside, but this man is happy, because things are OK inside. This happiness, says Jesus, belongs to the man who realizes his poverty in spirit.

POOR IN SPIRIT. Observe the two words, "IN SPIRIT." They take us at once, from the world of money into the realm of spiritual values. Jesus is NOT speaking of financial poverty here, but poverty of **personal righteousness**. Sinners by nature, all men deserve hell because of their sins (Rom. 3:23; 6:23). When a man compares his own holiness to God's holiness, he finds he is morally bankrupt. The person who RECOGNIZES THIS, says Jesus, is blessed. Why? It brings him before God in a spirit of brokenness, in deep humility. There is no pride in him, no self-reliance. This makes it possible for God to do for him what he can't do for himself — MAKE HIM AS RIGHTEOUS AS GOD (2 Cor. 5:21). That's why he's happy. INSIDE, he knows he's accepted by God, a blessedness all the money in the world can't buy. This then, is the beginning point, not only for salvation, but for the school of kings. The Christian must begin his spiritual life with this kind of humility and maintain it throughout his earthly life . . . all the way up the ladder.

KINGDOM OF HEAVEN. There are two families, you see. The family of the devil and the family of God. The devil is the ruler of this present world (2 Cor. 4:4). God rules the unseen world of the spirit (kingdom of heaven). The instant we're saved, our souls are immediately TRANSFERRED from Satan's family into God's family (Col. 1:13). Our bodies (flesh) continue to live in Satan's world, while our souls are citizens of heaven (Phil. 3:20). This makes for the fierce struggle of the Christian life. We have one foot on earth, and one foot in heaven, so to speak. When we receive Christ, a SECOND BIRTH occurs, a SPIRITUAL ONE. This new birth is what puts us in God's family. For the moment the kingdom of heaven is UNSEEN and will remain so until the last man to be saved has been plucked from the human stream. Then Jesus will return to take over the kingdoms of the world, establishing the kingdom of heaven on earth (Rev. 11:15). Our place in that kingdom will be determined by how well we do in the school of kings.

    4. Blessed are those who mourn (in spirit), for they shall be comforted.

matt. 5

MOURN. Since we live in the flesh, retaining our old natures after we're saved, we CONTINUE TO SIN. That old nature gives Satan access to our thoughts and feelings. He is able to insert terrible things in our minds — and we let him. This is why bad things often escape our lips and show up in our lives. That's not surprising says Emerson, since "the thought is father to the deed." Sigmund Freud was right to say the human mind "is a foul swamp." For here is where we sin. In our minds we bear anger, hatred, jealousy, greed and lust, along with bitterness and resentment. Recognizing this (poor in spirit) is one thing, how WE FEEL ABOUT IT is another. Do we MOURN our ugliness of spirit, or do we ignore it? Do we say the "blood of Jesus cleanses me from all sin," and then forget it? This is what the second rung of the ladder is all about. A blessedness awaits those who MOURN their poverty of spirit. For it is one thing to RECOGNIZE your foulness of spirit, quite another to CRY over it.

COMFORTED. Was the apostle Paul immune to lust and greed and jealousy, as well as unkind, unclean thoughts? He had an old nature too. Listen to him bewail its power to make him sin. **"I do not understand what I do. For what I want to do, I do not do, but what I hate I do . . . I know nothing good lives in me, that is in my sinful nature. For I have the desire to do what is good, but I cannot carry it out . . . "** (Rom. 7:15-18). Whipsawed by his two natures, the apostle cries out, "What a wretched man I am!" That's his mourning over his servitude to sin (vs. 25). He's pouring out his heart, yet in that same instant a wonderful thing happens — HE'S COMFORTED! "Thanks be to God," he says, "through Jesus Christ our Lord!" When we mourn our foulness, we empty ourselves. We pour out our hearts. Then God, beholding our self-emptying, fills us with Himself! Our feelings travel from deep mourning to the highest joy. We are comforted as God fill us with Himself! This truth is so important,

Jesus makes it the second rung of the ladder. If you've never thought it important to MOURN your inner ugliness, you know better now.

matt. 5

5. Blessed are the meek,
    for they will inherit the earth.

Meek. First, **meekness is not weakness.** Some picture the meek person as wishy-washy, a mamby-pamby Harvey Milktoast. Jesus is described as MEEK AND GENTLE. Yet He was surely a rugged man. Carpenters of those days had to be. Today, He would outwardly appear as a MACHO MAN, but

47

when you got to know Him, you'd find Him meek and gentle. But what is meek? Meekness is POWER UNDER CONTROL. With a whisper from the cross, Jesus could have consumed His enemies with fire. BUT HE RESTRAINED HIMSELF. Submitting to God's will, HE TOOK THE ABUSE. That's meekness. Climbing the BE-attitude ladder, you have already RECOGNIZED the inner ugliness of your old nature, MOURNING the filthiness of that brute. At this point, you don't mind sharing this LOW VIEW of yourself with God. But what about others? What if someone else agrees you're a rotten bum — and tells you so? Ah — the MEEK MAN doesn't mind. Compared to what he really deserves (HELL), he figures he's pretty well off. So he doesn't get angry should someone say, "Go to hell!" "Yeah, I should," he replies, "but thank God I won't." This man is RUGGED INSIDE. His anger and power are under control. He sits on that brute.

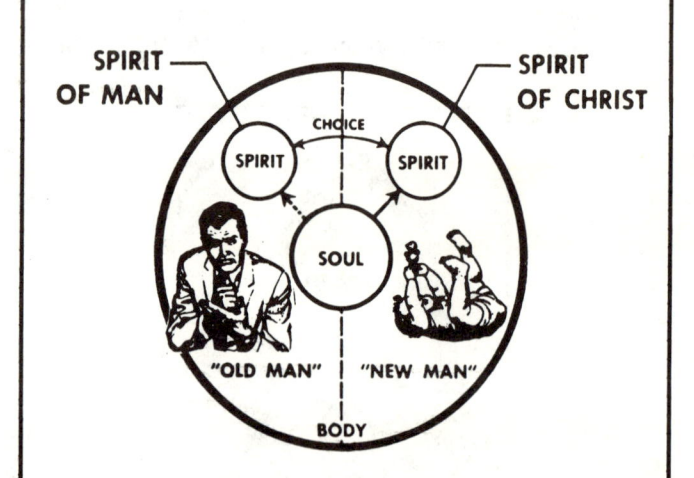

SPIRIT OF MAN — SPIRIT OF CHRIST

CHOICE

SPIRIT — SPIRIT

SOUL

"OLD MAN" — "NEW MAN"

BODY

See that old man? He's a brute, a filthy beast. Full of pride, selfishness and greed, he makes up the HUMAN SIDE of your character. In him is the burning desire for MORE. He is ready to stand up for his rights, insist on them, even strike or fight for them. He wants what's his. On the other side is the NEW MAN, your spiritual life, which is trying to GROW into the likeness of Christ. Just the OPPOSITE of the brute, he has power through Christ to overrule the desires of the OLD MAN. When he does, we call it SELF RESTRAINT or SELF CONTROL. The meek man restrains that beast, no matter what is said against him or what is done to him.

INHERIT. Christians can afford to be MEEK. So what if they don't get everything in this life — they're going to GET IT ALL, anyway. The meek ones will inherit the earth, says Jesus. Why contend or defend anything, when the entire world will be yours one day? "Inherit" points to that future day when Jesus returns to take over the kingdoms of this world (Rev. 11:15). We'll be with Him as "joint heirs" (Rom. 8:17). But how? Ah, by holding down HIGH RANKING JOBS in His administration. The meeker we are, the higher our rank. That's why we're climbing this ladder. So — it's worth it to sit on your feelings and watch what you do or say or think when someone puts you down or abuses you. It's vital not to react or get angry at anything, but be content to let God handle everything. How can anyone actually defraud you, when you're going to own the whole ball of wax!

6. Blessed are those who hunger and thirst for righteousness
    for they shall be filled.

HUNGER/THIRST. The Declaration of Independence lists among our inalienable rights, "life, liberty and the pursuit of happiness." Men pursue happiness or blessedness for all they're worth. They HUNGER for it, they THIRST for it. But it always escapes them. Seeking to satisfy their inner hunger, they try buying new houses, cars, taking trips, drugs, drinking, gambling, overeating, new jobs, new wives or husbands and moving to new locations. But nothing satisfies for long. Why? According to Jesus, happiness is not something you seek DIRECTLY. It comes as the BY-PRODUCT of seeking something else — RIGHTEOUSNESS. Many Christians are deceived about this. They seek to be blessed by going from meeting to meeting, experience to experience, seeking a filling of joy and ecstasy. But the Lord tells no one to do that. Believers are to hunger for righteousness. Righteousness is to the

matt. 5

soul, what food and water are to the body. They are to crave it like a man dying of thirst craves water. Only the Christian who is DESPERATE for righteousness will be filled with it.

Men pursue happiness or blessedness for all they're worth, but it always alludes them as they are looking in the wrong place.

RIGHTEOUSNESS. The Lord is called, "Jesus Christ the Righteous" (1st John 2:1). The righteousness we're to hunger for is the **likeness of the Lord,** i.e., to be like Him. In copying Jesus, we should ache to have in our lives only those things that please God, hating everything in us that doesn't. We should BURN with the desire to please God (John 8:29). We should HUNGER to see holiness and unselfishness blossom in our lives, along with a THIRST to give. But someone protests: "Hey! I thought Christ was our righteousness; that we're already the 'righteousness of God in Him!'" (2 Cor. 5:21). True — righteousness is something we HAVE in Christ, but it is also something we must CRAVE. How come? There are 3 stages of righteousness. The Bible calls them JUSTIFICATION, SANCTIFICATION, and GLORIFICATION. But if I draw them and re-name them, it will be easier to see how we can have God's righteousness and still hunger for it.

matt. 5

1. INSTANTANEOUS RIGHTEOUSNESS
The sinner at the moment of salvation

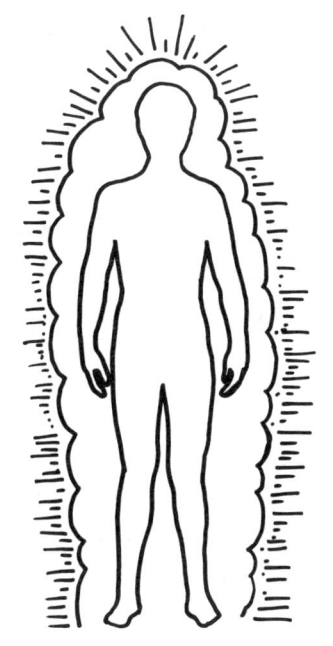

covered with God's righteousness

When we're saved, God instantly makes us as righteous as He, doing so by giving us His Spirit, which is holy. With His Spirit joined to our souls, we become as holy as He. This is how we RECEIVE righteousness. Ah — but we continue to sin, and will do so for as long as we remain in these bodies. God deals with this TEMPORARILY by covering us with a ROBE OF RIGHTEOUSNESS (Job 29:14; Rev. 19:8). Pictured by the robes of the Old Testament high priests, this robe conceals our sins. Thus it is possible for us to go into God's presence and not feel condemned. Atonement, a Hebrew word, means: "a covering."

matt. 5

Born to our mothers, we arrive in this world with a HUMAN NATURE, our old nature. When we're saved (born of God) we acquire another nature, the NEW NATURE. Thus we end up with a NEW MAN and an OLD MAN (Eph. 4:22-24). The new man, the result of having the Holy Spirit, is created in "righteousness and true holiness." Thus he is righteous. But he also NEEDS TO GROW, and when he does, it is called progressive righteousness. He won't grow, of course, unless he HUNGERS AND THIRSTS for righteousness. In placing the soul between two natures, God knows we'll FEEL THE POWER of sin AND SIN. It's guaranteed.

2. PROGRESSIVE RIGHTEOUSNESS

The believer with his two natures.

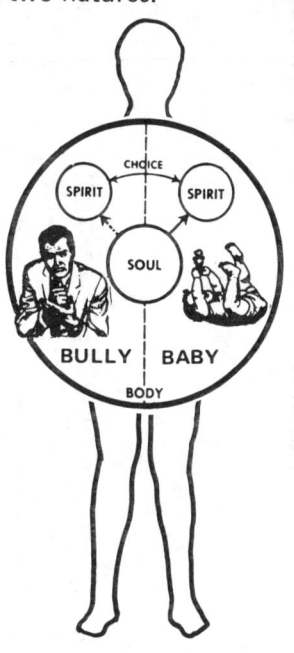

In this stage, the flesh (old man) WARS against the spirit (new man) (Gal. 5:17). And with that old man such a BULLY, Christians are shocked at how much they sin — at first. But for Christians to grow, this struggle is necessary. There's no way to OVERCOME without something to overcome. God wants us to RESIST EVIL, HATE IT, FIGHT IT, AND WIN. Every time we win, the new man grows more and more like Jesus. **That is growing in righteousness.** Only those who HUNGER AND THIRST after righteousness will fight hard against sin. During this stage, of course, when a believer is certain to sin, "there is NO CONDEMNATION to those who are in Christ Jesus" (Rom. 8:1). That's what the covering is for.

3. FUTURE RIGHTEOUSNESS

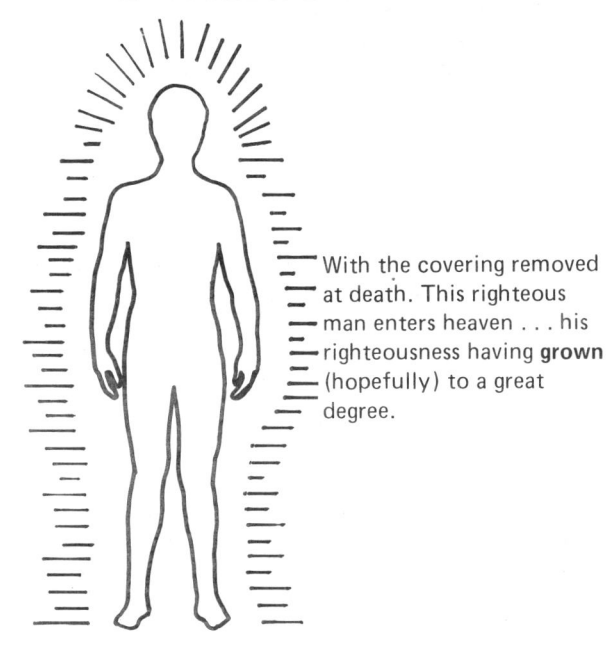

matt. 5

With the covering removed at death. This righteous man enters heaven ... his righteousness having **grown** (hopefully) to a great degree.

When the body is laid aside at physical death, SO IS THE OLD MAN. What's left? The NEW MAN **as he has grown in Christ**. With that old nature gone, the ROBE is no longer needed. The new man cannot sin (lst John 3:9). Born of God, he's as righteous as God. Ah — but how much did he GROW (progress) in Christlikeness? That's the BIG question. Yes, a righteous man CAN GROW in righteousness if he hungers and thirsts for it. Those who hunger the most, will display the greatest righteousness in heaven. While all Christians are righteous, they will certainly not all be EQUAL. How one handles the STEWARDSHIP of righteousness in this life, will count heavily at the judgment (Rom. 14:12). Growing in righteousness is part of the course for the SCHOOL OF KINGS. Our love for righteousness should increase every day. When it does, our CAPACITY for righteousness INCREASES also.

matt. 5

54

FILLED. Jesus says those with such a hunger will be FILLED. When? When we're with Jesus. All of us will be filled, but some will have BIGGER TANKS than others. Some will have a GREATER CAPACITY for righteousness. In what way will we be filled? In heaven we're going to EAT righteousness, SLEEP righteousness, even BREATHE IT. Righteousness is the ENVIRONMENT of heaven, **the only thing on the menu.** We should crave it now, because we're going to BE FILLED with it then. How awful to be filled with something for which you have no real desire! But how glorious to be filled with something you CRAVE! That's heavenly.

COMMENT: How does a Christian develop his capacity for righteousness? By STARVING the old man and FEEDING the new. The old man can be starved two ways: PHYSICALLY and MENTALLY. 1.) Go without food for 6 or 7 days and you'll behold something astonishing: the cries of your flesh (greed, sex, pride, hunger) WILL SUBSIDE and your spirit will **surface.** When you put Jesus AHEAD OF FOOD, the Lord becomes intensely real. Food is a god to many believers (Phil. 3:19). 2.) You can starve the old man MENTALLY by setting traps for Satan and catching him in the act

Food is a god to many believers, but when you put Jesus AHEAD OF FOOD, the Lord becomes intensely real.

matt. 5

of putting ideas in your mind. You see, he can drop ideas into your thought-stream and make you think THEY'RE YOUR OWN. That's power. But if you can DEFLECT the very first thoughts, you'll STOP FEEDING the old man — You'll STARVE HIM. As for the NEW MAN, he loves the Word of God. FEED HIM on the Word for 30 minutes a day and his growth will amaze you. The more you feed him, the more he CRAVES. In the process of doing this, your righteousness tank gets larger and larger.

7. Blessed are the merciful,
      for they shall obtain mercy.

MERCIFUL. With the 5th beatitude, other people now figure in our development. The first 4 beatitudes had to do with the way we SEE OURSELVES before God. If we see that OLD MAN as ugly and we are so BROKEN over his influence that it makes us MOURN; and this in turn makes us MEEK; and at the same time we're HUNGERING AND THIRSTING to be like Jesus — the natural by-product is being MERCIFUL TO OTHERS. But what is mercy? It is PITY IN ACTION. It is seeing another in a desperate situation and wanting to BRING RELIEF, **doing something** to ease the pain. Mercy is ASPIRIN for a wretched situation. Jesus is saying that any Christian who has climbed the LADDER this far, will have mercy showing up in his character. For you see, if the NEW MAN is growing at all, mercy has to show up in the life of that Christian.

ALREADY RECEIVED MERCY

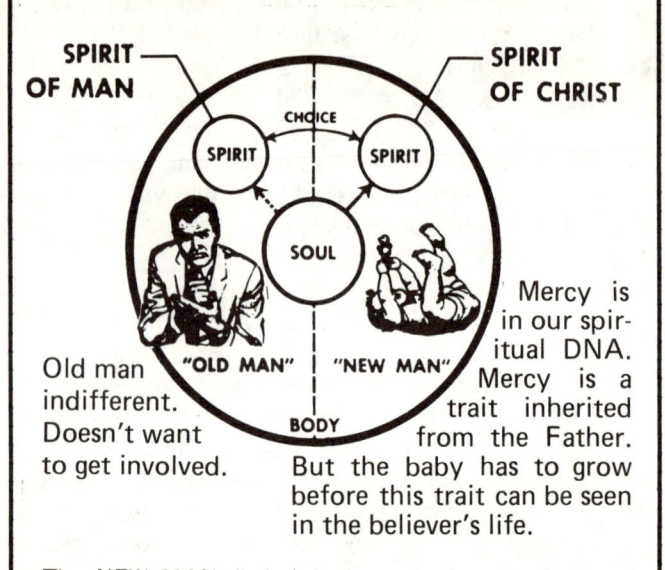

SPIRIT OF MAN — **SPIRIT OF CHRIST**

CHOICE · SPIRIT · SPIRIT · SOUL · "OLD MAN" · "NEW MAN" · BODY

Old man indifferent. Doesn't want to get involved.

Mercy is in our spiritual DNA. Mercy is a trait inherited from the Father. But the baby has to grow before this trait can be seen in the believer's life.

The NEW MAN (baby) is created when the Spirit of Christ is joined to our souls. This baby possesses in GERM FORM all the traits of its Father — GOD. Mercy is one of those traits — one which will show up in the Christian's life as the baby grows. When a developing Christian encounters a PITIFUL situation, his NEW MAN will want to jump in and help. It may be little help or a lot. But he won't totally ignore the awful plight of another when it is right under his nose. He's ready to DO SOMETHING even if it costs him a few dollars or inconveniences him. If it's a matter of forgiveness, he'll forgive. To the degree this Christian has grown in Christ, to that SAME DEGREE, he'll feel pity and help. Indifferent to the wretchedness of others, the OLD MAN doesn't want to get involved in misery and suffering. He might slow down to look at an accident, but he won't stop (as did the Good Samaritan). He might even give to the Red Cross. Worst of all, he will do all he can to keep the NEW MAN from showing mercy. That old man is like his father — Satan (John 8:44).

OBTAIN MERCY. Some read this beatitude and conclude, "If I'm not merciful to others, God will not forgive me and I won't go to heaven!" Later in the sermon, this idea is reinforced by similar words, "If you do not forgive men their sins, your heavenly Father will not forgive your sins" (Matt. 6:15). The truth is: Christians HAVE ALREADY RECEIVED MERCY. God took pity on us and "according to His mercy He saved us" (Titus 3:5). Therefore, salvation is NOT IN VIEW HERE. Even so, God's sons are expected to SHOW mercy. Why? Because of the HUGE DEBT OF SIN God has forgiven them (Matt. 18:35). In cancelling the GUILT of **all our sin**, God has wiped out far more than anyone could possibly owe us. Since He helped us in **our wretchedness**, we ought to show mercy to others in their wretchedness. It works like this — God has already shown mercy to us. Yet we STILL SIN and need mercy. By hardening our hearts, refusing to show mercy to others, we sin. Offended by this, God WILL NOT FORGIVE us until we CHANGE and show mercy. After apologizing to Him, He's glad to forgive us and restore us to fellowship. Our salvation is not involved in any way, since it is **fellowship** that is broken by this sin, not our **relationship** to God.

8. Blessed are the pure in heart,
   for they shall see God.

PURE. As we climb higher on the LADDER, we're learning more of what God expects of His PRINCES. We've now come to the heart. The Bible says much about the human heart — **all of it bad**. It is described as "deceitful above all things and desperately wicked" (Jer. 17:9). Nothing about it is pure. Out of it, says Jesus, come "evil thoughts, murder, adultery . . . etc" (Matt. 15:19). Even so, Jesus says ONLY THE PURE IN HEART will see God. With the human heart so impure, how can anyone ever hope to see God? A man can no more change his own heart, than a leopard can change its spots (Jer. 13:23). So how is such a thing possible? Ah — God has to GIVE US A NEW HEART. But how does He do that? The answer again brings us to the wonderful truth of the believer's two natures.

THE BELIEVER WITH HIS TWO NATURES

SPIRIT OF MAN — **SPIRIT OF CHRIST**

CHOICE — SPIRIT — SPIRIT — SOUL — "OLD MAN" — "NEW MAN" — BODY

Old man's heart is mean, selfish and continually evil.

Pure heart inherited from God. New creation (baby) is created "after God in righteousness and true holiness" (Eph. 4:22). As baby grows, this PURE HEART develops and appears in believer's life to be seen by others.

The NEW MAN is created WITH A PURE HEART. It's tiny, even embryonic, but nonetheless, pure. This BABY is just like God, with all of God's TRAITS built into it, though in GERM FORM. It has to grow. But it grows ONLY through struggle. This is why God places us between our two natures. This way we can exercise the BABY **through overcoming**. The NEW MAN will not grow apart from struggle. In physical conception, a fetus is complete, right down to the color of hair and eyes. This NEW CREATION is also complete, right down to the characteristics of its Father — GOD (Col. 2:10). A genuine, spiritual conception occurs when a man's soul is joined to God's Spirit. This is why the believer's heart is PURE, needing only to GROW.

HEART. What is the heart? it's not the muscle pumping blood through your body. The heart is where a man LIVES. No one lives in his arms or legs, BUT IN HIS MIND. Jesus, therefore, is talking about purity of one's thought-life. When you consider that powerful OLD NATURE is totally impure, you can see how difficult it is to have a pure mind. It's a FIGHT to keep evil out of one's thoughts. But if there's no fight, the mind remains evil continually. The more a person fights, the stronger the BABY HEART becomes. God sees to it that our days are filled with situations that give us plenty of opportunities to choose which heart we'll display. God wants PEOPLE to see our GROWING HEARTS, for that advertises the difference His Spirit makes in a man. The pure-hearted Christian does not lie, cheat, steal, exaggerate, nor grasp for the things of this world, knowing it's all going to be his one day. Later in the Sermon we'll see that the pure-hearted Christian is SALT to the world (5:13).

matt. 5

American Indians complained: "White man speak with forked tongue." Note the snake above. See his forked tongue. That pictures the believer's tongue, **a fork for each nature.** God does not want His children using double-talk, with hidden, unstated meanings and ulterior motives. With our two natures, evil can easily creep into what we think and say unless we are on guard. He wants our "YES" to mean yes and our "NO" to mean no. People dealing with single-hearted Christians should not have to read the fine print. They are up front with everything, knowing God's eyes behold their motives.

SEE GOD. Everyone is going to SEE GOD either as SAVIOR (at the judgment seat of Christ — 2 Cor. 5:10), or as JUDGE (at the great white throne — Rev. 20:11). So, when Jesus says . . . "SEE GOD," He obviously has more in mind than catching sight of God **as He really is.** Something special must be in store for the PURE IN HEART. Did you know that many Christians (perhaps most) are not too excited about seeing God? Why? They've spent their lives living for themselves and their families, with little time for Jesus. Instead of striving to be like Him, by fighting evil, they've drifted with the flow of the world. They could CRINGE at a face to face meeting with God. But it'll be different for the believer who has developed an INTIMATE FRIENDSHIP with the Lord through spending time with Him in the SECRET PLACE (Psa. 91:1). This believer has allowed the Lord's presence to become the BIGGEST THING in his life. Such a man is EAGER to meet the Lord face to face. When they meet, instead of hanging his head in shame, he'll rush into Jesus arms and they'll hug each other like two old friends getting together in the sky! (1 Thess. 4:17).

9. Blessed are the peacemakers,
for they shall be called the sons of God.

PEACE. Before we can discuss the PEACE-MAKER, we must discuss peace. Peace is something the world longs for, but cannot find. Why? It has to come from God. From the day Adam FELL in the garden of Eden, this world has not known peace. With that fall, Satan became the "god of this world" (2 Cor. 4:4). Doomed to an eternal hell, the devil's remaining delight is making life miserable for men and women (Matt. 25:41). He loves war, misery and all kinds of upheaval. Consequently peace VANISHED from this planet when Satan took over. If there is to be peace for anyone, it must come from the GOD OF

PEACE. Satan is the god of trouble and unrest. Our Lord is the GOD OF PEACE (Rom. 15:33; Rom. 16:20, 2 Cor. 13:11; 1 Thess. 5:23; Heb. 13:20). With God the source of peace, no one is going to have genuine peace apart from Him. Peace is simply not available except as it comes through God's servants acting as peacemakers.

THE PEACEMAKER AND HIS TWO NATURES.

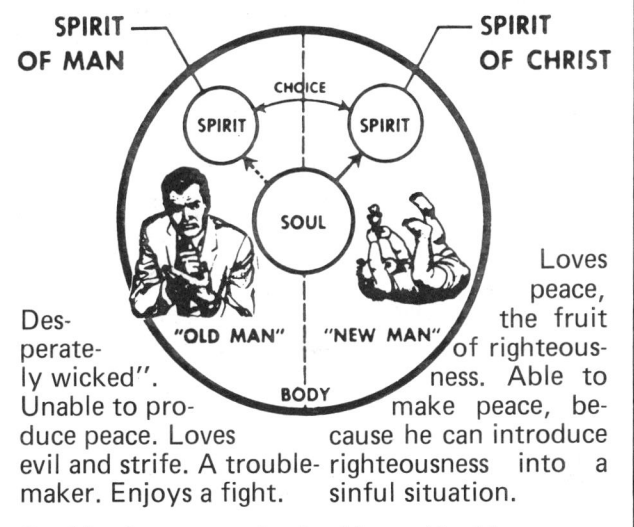

SPIRIT OF MAN — **SPIRIT OF CHRIST**

CHOICE
SPIRIT — SPIRIT
SOUL
"OLD MAN" | "NEW MAN"
BODY

"Desperately wicked". Unable to produce peace. Loves evil and strife. A troublemaker. Enjoys a fight.

Loves peace, the fruit of righteousness. Able to make peace, because he can introduce righteousness into a sinful situation.

Consider how we arrive in this world with a nature BENT ON TROUBLE. Wars, strife, unrest flow naturally from the OLD NATURE, that wicked human heart. The unsaved, having ONLY the OLD MAN, cannot make peace. They might declare a truce from time to time, but wars keep coming and human life is saturated with trouble. The NEW MAN, on the other hand, conceived by the "GOD OF PEACE," loves peace. Created "after God," in righteousness, there is NO SIN in him. It is SIN that brings trouble to people. Replace that sin with righteousness and trouble vanishes. Only a child of God can introduce righteousness into a situation. No one else has it.

matt. 5

PEACEMAKER. Nations seek to settle disputes with weapons. "BLAST your enemies" is the world's way. But getting rid of an enemy is not true peace. Peace has to do with RECONCILING two opposing parties. When a peacemaker steps in with a righteous solution, and both parties are happy with that solution and embrace each other, THAT IS REAL PEACE. Peace is not a truce. Real peace comes when the warring parties have a change of heart and "kiss and make up." Only the NEW MAN can do this, for only he has a heart for it. The OLD MAN would rather see a quarrel. A peacemaker is a Christian who HAS GROWN to the place where he HATES quarrelling and feels COMPELLED to step in and do what he can to reconcile hostile parties. That is why this beatitude is so high on the LADDER. Until one has climbed this far, he does not have a peacemakers heart. When a man on the 7th rung sees trouble brewing, everything in him says, "I must see what I can do to end this conflict and prevent further strife."

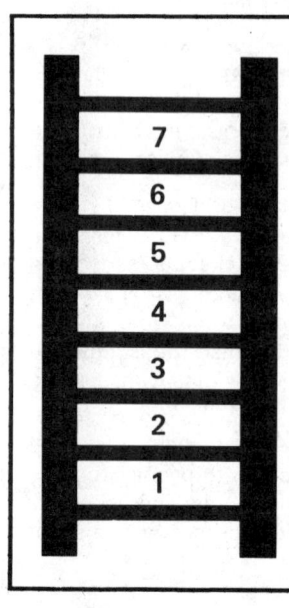

Observe how high we've come. This is high altitude stuff. To be a peacemaker, one must climb the first six steps. He must see the blackness of his own heart and know the power of that old nature. Aware that it makes people fight, he hates it. What's more, he's meek about it and full of mercy as he beholds the warring parties. His own hunger for righteousness makes him EAGER to step in, regardless of risk, to do what he can to make peace. Only those who've reached this high level will have such a passion and at the same time possess sufficient pity and neutrality to handle it. Clearly it takes a man on the 7th rung.

matt. 5

SON OF GOD. What's the peacemaker's reward? He gets called a name — SON OF GOD. When people see you doing what the GOD OF PEACE does, they conclude — LIKE FATHER, LIKE SON. You're recognized as being His. Sometimes the term SON OF GOD is meant kindly, other times it is not. Not infrequently, the very people you're trying to help will turn on you. They don't appreciate your efforts at all. But that must not dampen your spirit. Jesus, as you know, stepped in to settle the trouble between God and man and was crucified for His efforts. Moses was run off for trying to settle strife between two struggling Hebrews (Ex. 2:11-15). So, acting like God is not always easy. There can be a price to pay. On the other hand, it THRILLS GOD to see you doing what He does — just to please Him. While others may not always appreciate your efforts, God smiles and says, "That's my boy! That's my girl!"

10. Blessed are those who are persecuted for the sake of righteousness,
 for the kingdom of heaven is theirs.

PERSECUTED. We've come to the top of the ladder, a good place to remind ourselves that believers live by a DIFFERENT SET OF RULES totally opposite from the ways of the world. And if we live by those rules, we are GOING TO BE DIFFERENT, A DIFFERENCE THAT is certain to bring persecution. The more we live by the RULES OF THE KINGDOM (The Sermon on the Mount), the more we become like Jesus. And the more we become like Him, the more the world will hate us. He made that plain enough, "If they persecuted Me, they'll persecute you also" (John 15:20). Because of His personal righteousness, the Lord had a CONDEMNING EFFECT on the self-righteous ones around Him. The Pharisees especially hated Him, because He made all their "good works" look bad when compared with His. The effect was

INTRO B

such they couldn't stand to have Him around. They finally murdered Him. As we become more like Him, we can expect the same thing.

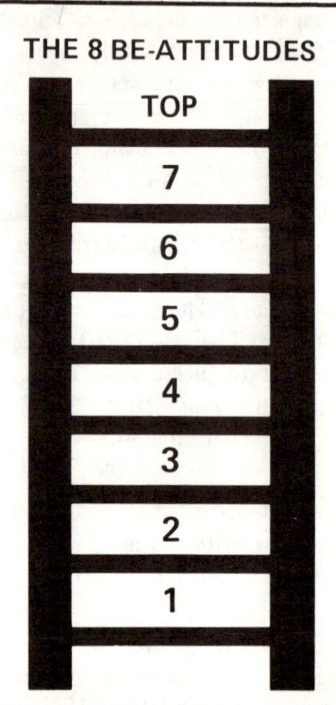

THE 8 BE-ATTITUDES

```
         TOP
          7
          6
          5
          4
          3
          2
          1
```

Being on TOP OF THE LADDER is risky, even precarious. It's dangerous to become LIKE CHRIST in this hostile world, a world which hates Him. That might not seem believeable in America, where RELIGIOUS FREEDOM (all kinds) is regarded as a basic right. Yet, even here one can lose his job and be exposed to ridicule, if he becomes too much like Jesus. But as for being tortured and killed — that can't happen here, yet. In other parts of the world, however, believers are being slaughtered for righteousness sake this very moment. Signs are mounting that our freedoms may not last much longer. Once they're gone, being like Jesus could easily mean martyrdom. When that happens, this could be the most important verse in our lives.

matt. 5

RIGHTEOUSNESS. It's easy to be confused about suffering for righteousness' sake. When life is terribly hard, some feel that is persecution. That the stress of their circumstances is due to their righteousness. But it's not so. Others are FOOLISH with their TESTIMONY. Lacking tact or wisdom, they make pests of themselves to the place where people run them off. Then they rejoice, thinking they've suffered for righteousness' sake. Then there are those who get involved in noble causes such as anti-abortion and anti-communism. When they're blasted for their zealous actions, they feel they are suffering for righteousness. But the ONLY TIME persecution is **blessed**, is when people hate you BECAUSE OF JESUS. The Lord confirms this in verse 11, where He substitutes the words, "BECAUSE OF ME." That's the righteousness He's talking about. Therefore to suffer for righteousness' sake, means to be persecuted because you are SO LIKE CHRIST, that you condemn the evil in those around you and they hate you for it.

KINGDOM. When a believer is faced with the loss of everything, even his life — because he is like Jesus — it's fabulous to know the **kingdom is his**. This doesn't mean simply entering the kingdom, but that it BELONGS to him. Even as the blows are falling, he KNOWS his place in heaven is secure. The very blows themselves are a testimony or badge certifying his future. Beyond that, all the treasure he has laid up (Matt. 6:20), as well as his future job with Jesus, are assured. He may lose everything on earth, but nothing can touch what God has sealed for him in heaven. That's why a Christian can rejoice when he's persecuted for righteousness' sake. He's so much like His Lord, God is thrilled with Him and GUARANTEES him the best of heaven. Those suffering persecution, BECAUSE OF JESUS, belong to a select group. Not only have they climbed to the top of the ladder, but they are certain to be among the RICH AND FAMOUS of eternity.

matt. 5

NOTE. At this point, the Lord makes an interesting departure — He comments on the eighth beatitude. He did not expand any of the other seven beatitudes, but the following two verses are His commentary on the idea of being persecuted for righteousness sake.

11. Blessed are you when people insult you, persecute you and make all kinds of false statements about you, because of Me. Accept it joyfully. Yes, even leap with ecstasy, because your reward in heaven is so great! It will be as great as any of the prophets who were before you, for they were persecuted in the same way.

"If the world hates you," said Jesus to His disciples just hours before the cross, "bear in mind it hated Me first. If you belonged to the world, it would treat you as one of its own. But since I have chosen you out of the world, so that you no longer belong to it, the world will hate you" (John 15:18-19). While our land has enjoyed religious freedom for some 400 years, signs mount that a change is just ahead. The day is swiftly approaching when it's going to be rough to be a Christian. In that day, standing up for Jesus will almost certainly mean death.

BECAUSE OF ME. In the last beatitude the Lord speaks of suffering "BECAUSE OF RIGHTEOUSNESS," but here He makes that parallel to "BECAUSE OF ME." It is clear now: He is speaking of a life that DISPLAYS His righteousness, not the mere profession of being a Christian. And it's the kind of a life that invites persecution, because the believer is SO MUCH LIKE JESUS. The Lord widens the persecution to include INSULTS and the SPREADING OF TERRIBLE LIES. Under this type of persecution it's hard to survive. A person can lose his job, have his reputation ruined and be put out of business. Should this surprise us? No. The Lord has already made it plain that we are to be His WITNESSES (Acts 1:8). In Greek the word for witnesses is — **MARTYRS!** When you live in a world that hates Christ, you put your life on the line when you stand up for Him. The abuse He describes can be expected by anyone who displays His kind of righteousness.

LEAP WITH ECSTASY. The Lord gives a COMMAND as to how we're to face any persecution coming against us. The command is to ACCEPT IT WITH JOY — even leap for joy. Implied in Jesus' command are three specifics: 1.) Don't retaliate, 2.) Don't say one word against your persecutors, 3.) Don't even harbor resentment against them. Really? Is that true? Yes, for you see it is impossible to harbor resentment and strike back while you're REJOICING. Now your OLD MAN says, "Just let someone try breaking into my house to seize my family. I'll go down fighting before I'll let that happen!" Ah, but the NEW MAN, who views persecution for Jesus' sake as PROOF OF HIS SONSHIP, says, "Lord Jesus, I believe You when You say I am BLESSED because of this persecution!" Who can do such a thing? Only someone who has reached the TOP OF THE LADDER; someone whose NEW MAN has been nurtured and developed for such a moment. It is urgent that we all get busy and climb the ladder, for the hour of persecution approaches.

matt. 5

REWARD. You've heard some say, "I don't want to serve Jesus for any reward. I want to serve Him out of love." Jesus, however, understands HUMAN MOTIVATION better than we. This is HIS WORD on the matter. He says we can rejoice in a persecution situation if we KEEP OUR EYES ON OUR HEAVENLY REWARD. The writer to the Hebrews tell us that JESUS HIMSELF was motivated by reward. He endured the cross and its shame, says the writer, because of the JOY SET BEFORE HIM (Heb. 12:2). Moses tossed aside the wealth of Egypt to bear the reproach of Christ, because he had HIS EYES ON THE REWARD (Heb. 11:25-27). Christians should fix their eyes on their GOAL, not on their immediate circumstances. Every student should be motivated by the thought of GRADUATION and what lies beyond. Why go through the SCHOOL OF KINGS unless your ambition is to reign with Christ! God has undreamed pleasures and treasures reserved for His faithful ones — and He offers them as MOTIVATION. What's more says Jesus, suffering this kind of persecution makes you part of a most celebrated company — THE PROPHETS. To be in that group, would make you one of the BIG SHOTS of heaven! After all, you're being groomed for a throne!

"Now that we know what it takes to be a BEATITUDE MAN or BEATITUDE WOMAN, what does God expect of us? When we climb the beatitude-ladder and become more like Christ, what does the Lord intend to do with us?"

13. You are the salt of the world. But if salt loses its salty character, can it be made salty again? No, it has become totally useless and is thrown out and people trample on it.

WORLD. Christianity is NOT a monastery. There's nothing private about belonging to Jesus. It is a public matter — and for good reason. As believers ascend the BEATITUDE LADDER, becoming more and more like Jesus, their **character** is VERY DIFFERENT from the world. This difference is useful to the Lord, for it has a powerful effect on the world. This is why He sends us INTO THE WORLD, rather than into isolated cells, secluded and shielded from the world (Matt. 28:19). He wants our difference to IMPACT the world. Nowhere does He teach we can CHANGE the world, only that we can have a telling effect on it. To describe the effect TRANSFORMED BELIEVERS have on the world, Jesus uses two metaphors — SALT AND LIGHT.

SALT. Salt has two prime uses: 1.) it can make foods taste better, 2.) it is a preservative. No way are we to understand Jesus as saying we are to make this world taste better to God. It's so corrupt and rotten, no amount of salt could make it taste good to Him. But as a PRESERVATIVE, Christian salt has a SLOWING EFFECT on the decay of the world. This is what Jesus has in mind. With believers living out their righteousness, they become a SALT that slows down the decaying process. When you consider that prison reforms, hospitals, the abolition of slavery, anti-abortion and a host of other benefits have come through caring Christians, the slowing effect is not hard to see. A beatitude Christian who pays his bills, keeps his word, refuses to steal from his employer, never retaliates, resists off color jokes and is transparently honest in his dealing — is SO DIFFERENT from those around him, he makes an impact. A goodly number living for Christ, can definitely slow down the putrifying of the world.

THROWN OUT. When Jesus speaks of salt losing its salty character, He is referring to Christians who are NO DIFFERENT from the world — those NOT CLIMBING the ladder. The only way any Christian can become truly different is by climbing the BEATITUDE LADDER. The great shame of modern

matt. 5

Christianity is the **lack of difference** between believers and non-believers **in the way they live**. To be useful to the Lord, the Christian MUST BE DIFFERENT — that's what makes him SALT. But if he chooses to live for himself and his family, rather than climbing the ladder, there's no way he can be SALT. No difference equals no salt. As you know, when things are useless, they're thrown out as trash. Jesus is not saying UNSALTY Christians will be thrown out of the kingdom, but He will surely wash them out of the school of kings. In the more humble areas of the Orient, waste baskets aren't needed. People simply open their doors and sweep everything into the streets where pedestrians trample it.

"If our difference is SALT, what is our LIGHT?"

14. You are the light of the world. A city atop a hill cannot be hidden. 15. When men light a lamp, they don't put it under a tub, do they? No, they put it on a lamp-stand that it might provide light for everyone in the house. 16. You're to be like that, letting your light so shine that people can see your good deeds and give the credit to your Father in heaven.

LIGHT. If the beatitude-Christian's CHARACTER is salt, what is HIS LIGHT? Well, what is God's light? **His Word.** "The entrance of Thy words, O lord, bringeth light" (Psa. 119:130). Again, "Thy word is a lamp unto my feet, and a light unto my path" (Psa. 119:105). If God's Word is His light, what is the Christian's light? HIS WORD. Words provide INSIGHT, spiritual light. There's no way to obtain spiritual light apart from words, whether spoken or printed on paper. For a Christian to BE LIGHT, He must give out words. But what does his light shine on? Ah. his character, his good deeds. If he doesn't shine his light like this, men will look at his good deeds and his difference, notice how different he is, and GIVE HIM THE CREDIT. They will never credit God with those good deeds, for it won't occur to them. Since they do not know God, nor care to hear about Him, they will always credit the beatitude-Christian, rather than his heavenly Father.

matt. 5

Light = Words

"The **Lord** loves you and has sent me to help you."

THE BELIEVER'S LIGHT SHINING ON HIS DEEDS

Salt = Deeds (Character)

See how the believer's LIGHT illuminates his DEEDS. They are not the same. One illuminates the other. Because of spiritual darkness, the world has no way of knowing a believer is different because of Christ. Therefore the believer MUST TELL HIM. When a BEATITUDE-MAN says, "I am what I am because of Jesus," his light is shining on his character. Once a person hears those words he is FORCED to connect the Christian with God and glorify Him. That is, credit Him for the difference. If God's man does NOT SPEAK, then God is left out. The Christian will get the credit. In a spiritually dark world, there is no way for spiritual truths to be seen without spiritual light (words).

matt. 5

CITY ON A HILL. Jesus is thinking of night travelers, journeying in the dark, with only the flickering lights of cities to guide them. In those days, cities were built atop hills for protection and their faint glow could be seen in the distance. The unsaved are like that, traveling in the spiritual darkness of this world. When a BEATITUDE-CHRISTIAN speaks, even a few words will give off spiritual light. Like a city on a hill, the faint glimmer makes it possible for a person to see a WAY OUT of this stinking, dying world and be saved. If someone asks, "How are you?" A faint glow is seen when you reply, "Great! With the Lord taking care of me, how can I feel otherwise!" If a hungry heart asks that question, those few words will open the door. But to withhold such a tiny bit of light, is like putting a lamp under a tub. That makes no sense. A light has to be displayed where people can see by it. If it isn't they will surely stumble and fall.

"Is there anything else the Lord wants to make clear before He applies the beatitudes to specific situations?"

17. Don't think for a minute that I have come to abolish the law or the prophets, because I haven't. To the contrary, I have come to fulfill the entire law, right down to the smallest letter, yes, even the tiniest flick of the pen. 18. Be assured that as long as heaven and earth stand, the law will remain in full force.

"Wait a minute! Why is He talking to Christians about the law

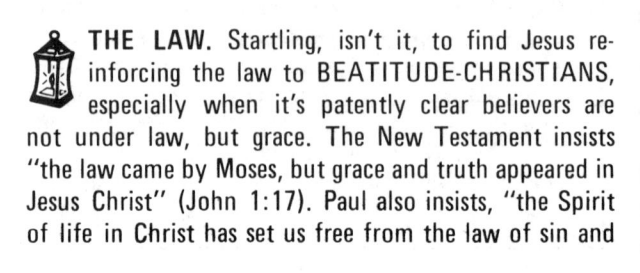

THE LAW. Startling, isn't it, to find Jesus reinforcing the law to BEATITUDE-CHRISTIANS, especially when it's patently clear believers are not under law, but grace. The New Testament insists "the law came by Moses, but grace and truth appeared in Jesus Christ" (John 1:17). Paul also insists, "the Spirit of life in Christ has set us free from the law of sin and death" (Rom. 8:2). So what is Jesus' point? It's this — the grace of God does NOT ERASE the law. The Lord is about to teach His disciples that salvation by faith does NOT CANCEL the believer's obligatin to keep the law. Why? Because the LAW is the **standard of perfection** for God's kingdom, the very kingdom into which we're born when we're saved. That standard is the righteousness of God. No believer should react against that, for this is what the beatitudes seek to produce in our lives. The very thing for which BEATITUDE-PEOPLE hunger and thirst — is the righteousness of God.

THE STANDARD OF RIGHTEOUSNESS

When Jesus speaks of the LAW AND THE PROPHETS, He is referring to that STANDARD OF RIGHTEOUSNESS God gave His people Israel through Moses. It consisted of the 10 commandments and all the moral principles that flowed from them. It included all the LEGISLATIVE RULES that governed the nation as well as the SACRIFICIAL SYSTEM (temple program). Clearly He is referring to the entire OLD TESTAMENT LAW. NOT A SPECK of this law, says Jesus, is abolished by His coming. Instead, it is **fullfilled**. God, being God, could not set any standard of righteousness LESS THAN HIS OWN. Jesus would NEVER do away with that! He Himself is the righteousness of God. (1 Cor. 1:30).

matt. 5

DON'T THINK. When you see Jesus picking corn on the sabbath and healing people, one could get the idea He was deliberately going against the law of Moses. But He wasn't. He was going against the law of the Pharisees and teachers of the law. These teachers made a great show of KEEPING the law, but what they were keeping was a WATERED DOWN EDITION of the law of Moses. They couldn't live up to the PERFECTION required by the law, so they REDUCED its requirements, limiting the law to OUTWARD ACTS. To them, if a man did not go to bed with his neighbor's wife, he'd not broken the law. And if he had not actually slain another person, he had kept that part of the law. This is why the rich young ruler could say . . . "All these things have I kept from my youth . . . " (Mk. 10:17ff.) In the Pharisee mind this was true, but it was a long way from the REAL MEANING of God's law. This is what Jesus is going to make clear. He comes on the scene as the TRUE INTERPRETER of God's law. He's going to explain it to His BEATITUDE-PEOPLE as God meant for it to be understood. He is going to do it by CONTRASTING how God views the law, with what the Pharisees and teachers were giving the people.

19. Anyone who seeks to diminish even the least requirement of the law and teaches others to do the same, will be called least in the kingdom of heaven. And anyone who practices the real meaning of its commands and teaches others to live by them, will be called great in the kingdom of heaven.

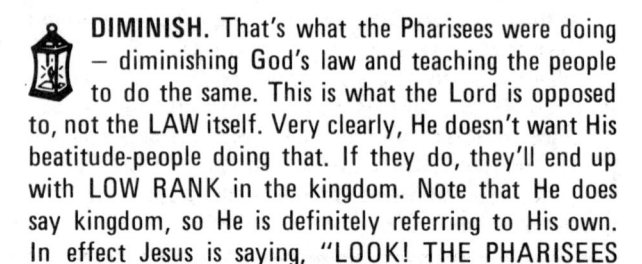

DIMINISH. That's what the Pharisees were doing — diminishing God's law and teaching the people to do the same. This is what the Lord is opposed to, not the LAW itself. Very clearly, He doesn't want His beatitude-people doing that. If they do, they'll end up with LOW RANK in the kingdom. Note that He does say kingdom, so He is definitely referring to His own. In effect Jesus is saying, "LOOK! THE PHARISEES

ARE WRONG ABOUT THE LAW! THE BEATITUDES ARE THE REAL LAW, AS GOD MEANT FOR IT TO BE UNDERSTOOD FROM THE BEGINNING." The Pharisees/doctors were teaching it was legal to divorce your wife for **any reason**. And if someone put out your eye, you had a right to put out his eye. In this manner, they diminished the law. The REAL LAW, says Jesus, is the righteousness of God and it will stand for all time. Therefore it not only applies to the Old Testament people, but to His disciples as well. But that shouldn't bother beatitude-people. After all, the beatitudes set forth the TRUE MEANING of the law — Jesus' own righteousness.

A GRAPHIC VIEW OF CHAPTER FIVE

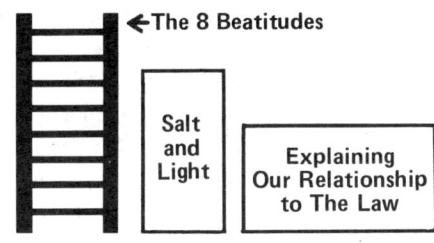

← The 8 Beatitudes

Salt and Light

Explaining Our Relationship to The Law

6 Items of The Law Explained by Jesus

The 8 beatitudes, first of all, make up the basic course for the school of kings. Involved in this course, we become totally different from the world in the way we live. This makes us SALT. But for God to get the credit for our changed lives, we must shine our LIGHT (words) on our works so people will see HIM as the cause of our different behavior. Before the Lord moves on to specific applications of the beatitudes, He wants us to understand our relationship to the law of Moses. So for the rest of chapter 5, He will take up 6 ITEMS OF LAW and give the correct interpretation. In no way is He quarrelling with the law. He is simply exposing the FALSE IN—TERPRETATION the Jewish teachers were placing on it. Believers, hungering and thirsting for righteousness, need to know what God expects of them, before they can live such a life and teach others to do the same.

matt. 5

REAL MEANING. While the Pharisees limited the law to actual murder and adultery, etc., Jesus will show the TRUE MEANING of the law has to do with one's heart and feelings. The law has to do with attitudes. Adultery, Jesus will say, is not limited to illicit affairs, but the lustful look of the eye and the UNCLEAN THOUGHTS of the imagination. He will show that MURDER, far from being limited to the slaying of another, has to do with ANGRY THOUGHTS about another and letting ANGRY WORDS come from your lips. And when you DISLIKE certain people and PREFER others, you are breaking God's law. All these have to do with FEELINGS of the heart — attitudes of the heart. For it is in their hearts that men sin, not in their bodies. The law of God really applies to THE HEART, not the outward act. Men don't sin in their bodies. For as Emerson said, "The thought is father to the deed." What men do in the flesh is simply the carrying out of what's in their hearts. The heart is where the law of God is directed, as Jesus will make very clear.

20. Hear me carefully, for unless your righteousness surpasses that of the Pharisees and doctors of the law, you cannot possibly enter the kingdom of heaven.

SURPASSES: What a bombshell! Jesus' listeners were stunned. They looked at each other in amazement. Heads shook. Eyes blinked. "How can we be more righteous than our leaders!" they asked. "You'd better," replied Jesus, "or there'll be no place for you in heaven!" Of course He was speaking of a **different kind** of righteousness. He was speaking of HEART-RIGHTEOUSNESS, the kind that comes by faith. The Pharisees and doctors knew nothing of this righteousness, but Moses did. So did David and the prophets. Consequently, the very ones responsible for educating the people, were actually teaching them to live FAR BELOW God's standard. This was why the Lord rebuked Nicodemus. As THE TEACHER (supt. of education for Israel), he should have known that righteousness comes BY FAITH. And that God's plan called for the HOLY SPIRIT to write the LAW (true meaning) on men's hearts. Nicodemus' ignorance was exposed when he didn't know what Jesus was talking about when He said, "a man has to be born again (from above) even to see the kingdom of God!" (John 3:3).

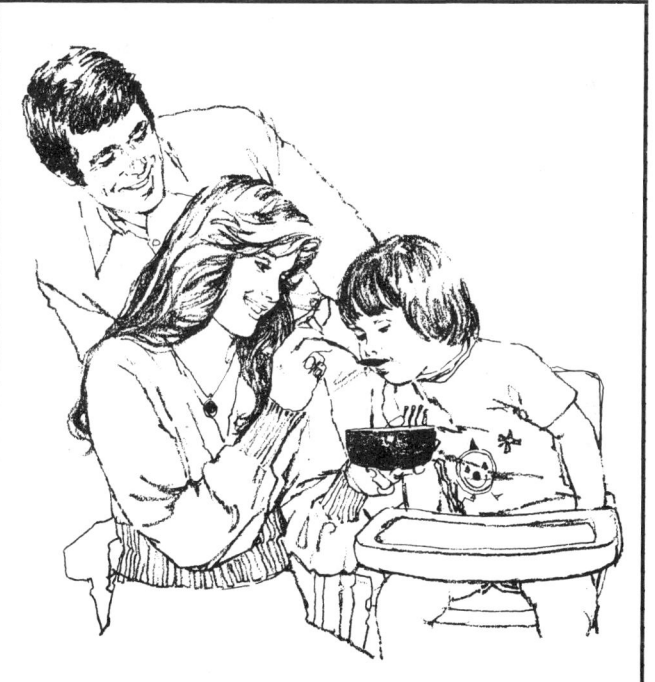

matt. 5

77

See the pains those parents are taking to feed their little one? Without food he wouldn't grow at all. Similarly, the believer must feed on God's Word daily. It is the only spiritual food. By refusing to feed the OLD MAN and purposing to feed only the NEW MAN, our lives gradually change into the likeness of Christ.

matt. 5

YOUR RIGHTEOUSNESS. Though we BECOME righteous when we're saved, that righteousness is NOT SEEN by others until we become BEATITUDE MEN AND WOMEN. As we climb the beatitude-ladder, becoming more and more like Jesus, we start displaying OUR RIGHTEOUSNESS, the righteousness of the NEW MAN. But that's not easily done. It's hard work, a terrible fight, STARVING the old man and FEEDING the new. But as we TRY, we gradually make changes into the likeness of the Lord (2 Cor. 3:18). Then our righteousness becomes increasingly visible. Believe it or not, this very process is LIVING THE LAW. For you see, GOD IS NOT A LAWYER, HE'S A FATHER. He doesn't keep track of our failures, for He knows the evil in us makes for lots of failures. He keeps track of our PROGRESS, for with Him — TRYING IS WINNING. Now for the most exciting truth in all this discussion: when we TRY to be what God wants us to be, to Him — THAT'S THE SAME AS KEEPING THE LAW. For the LAW has to do with the heart, and in our hearts we "hunger and thirst" for the righteousness

> God is not a lawyer. He's a Father. He doesn't keep track of our failures.

of the law. We ache to be like Jesus. That's the bottom line of the whole law — being like Jesus.

"Will Jesus explain how the law should be understood? Will He give us an example of what He means by the true interpretation of the law?"

21. As you know, our people have been told for centuries, **"Do not commit murder"** and anyone who does commit murder, must answer to the judge. 22. But I tell you that anyone who is angry with his brother will face judgment. And whoever calls his brother "a stupid jerk" will be brought before the supreme court. And anyone who says to his brother, "you dirty rat," faces the fires of hell.

Murder. For His first explanation of the law's true meaning, Jesus selects the 6th commandment, "Do not commit murder." Murders are planned, involving a decision of the heart. That's what God sees. And that's where the law is aimed. But as far as the Pharisees and the doctors of the law were concerned, the commandment was NOT BROKEN until someone had been killed. They reasoned, much like our modern police, "You can't arrest a man for what he's thinking!" Jesus corrects that notion. "But I say unto you . . . ," He says, declaring ANGER, SPITE AND CONTEMPT, all of which occur in the heart, break the 6th commandment. He moves through the whole Jewish justice concept — the court (the judge), the supreme court (the Sanhedrin) and finally hell, to show that it is the HEART ATTITUDE that condemns men in God's eyes. Makes sense, for it is also the HEART ATTITUDE that sends men to heaven. To say "stupid jerk" insults one's **intelligence,** and "dirty rat" maligns his **character.** In effect Jesus is saying, "anytime you're angry with someone, because of something he's said or done to you, you're sinning in God's sight as surely as the murderer.

matt. 5

JESUS' TEACHING VERSUS PHARISEES' TEACHING

Pharisees
Unless you actually kill a man, you have not broken the 6th commandment.

Jesus
When you become ANGRY with another person for something said or done that offends you, you HAVE broken the 6th commandment.

"God sees not as a man sees," said Samuel the prophet. "For man looks on the outward appearance, but God looks on the heart" (1 Sam. 16:7). Consequently, God's LAW is based on what HE SEES, not on what man sees. True, the police can't arrest you for what you're thinking — they can't read your heart. Therefore man's law has to be limited to OUTWARD ACTS. This is what the Pharisees sought to do with God's law, insisting people did not sin until a physical act was committed. But Jesus says the Pharisees are wrong. That God's law applies to WHAT HE SEES and that in His eyes — THE THOUGHT IS THE SAME AS THE DEED.

ANGRY. "Wait a minute!" you say, "Jesus got angry, didn't He!" And how. When He saw those money changers and cattle auctioneers in the temple court, He was furious (John 2:13-17). He was consumed with anger. But please note it was NOT FOR HIS OWN SAKE, He was zealous for God's house. There is a place for anger if it's aimed at SIN, at our own evil natures, or at Satan. But there is no place for anger when someone offends us, upsets us or displeases us.

matt. 5

Anger is the devil's territory. When we're angry, terrible things arise in our minds and issue from our mouths — all set on fire of hell (Ja. 3:6; Matt. 15:18,19). This is why the apostle John said, "He that hates his brother is a murderer" (1st John 3:15). MURDER IS ANGER IN ACTION. When Jesus was personally abused (beaten, spit upon, crucified), He didn't retaliate. Instead, He said, "Father forgive them." We have a long way to go, don't we?

"How about some practical illustrations that will let us see how Jesus' interpretation of the law works in real life."

23. So when you're bringing your gift to the altar and suddenly remember your brother has a grievance against you, 24. stop what you're doing. Leave your gift right where it is. Go immediately and make things right with your brother and then come back and offer your gift.

STOP. Presented in modern terms, the Lord's first illustration has to do with church. You're sitting in your seat, when suddenly you think of someone you've offended and who is upset with you. Get out of your seat at once, says Jesus. Go and be reconciled to your brother. To the Lord, it is more important to heal that situation than to remain in church — even if you're in the midst of offering Him praise. To sit there, aware of the injured relationship, makes a sham of being in church. Therefore His "GO" is URGENT. The devil could exploit the situation into an awful mess if you dally, leading you to sin even worse than you are already. This is an area where BEATITUDE-PEOPLE must not **drag their feet.** It's something that can seriously hinder their progress in the school of kings. So here's the big lesson: every angry thought, angry word, or angry look that hurts others, is **the same as murder in God's eyes.** If you didn't know that before, you do now and directly from the Lord.

matt. 5

25. If someone brings suit against you, come to terms with him quickly before the court date. Make an out-of-court settlement while you have the chance, otherwise he might win the case and the judge will hand you over to the jailer and you'll be thrown into prison. Think of the feelings that would boil within you if you had to stay in there until the last penny was paid.

SETTLE. Jesus' second illustration has to do with someone so upset with you, he takes you to court. Jesus says, when you have an enemy like that, "DONT WAIT UNTIL IT GETS TO COURT. SETTLE IT BEFOREHAND." And He means, even when you think the suit is unfair. It may cost you dollars to settle, but that's better, says the Lord, than having satanic feelings raging inside you as time drags on. Court battles create a field day for the devil. No matter how much it costs to settle, the loss will be nothing compared to the spiritual ground you'll lose stewing about the situation. Again it is a matter of THE HEART, for that is where you break the law and sin against God. Jesus would spare us that. He wants us to WIN out over our old natures. And we can if we'll put pleasing God ahead of money. Beatitude-people have to be committed to SELF-CONTROL and that means avoiding such situations, no matter the cost.

"How about a sensitive matter like adultery? Will the Lord show us how the true interpretation of the law applies to that?

27. Again and again you've been told, **"Do not commit adultery."** 28. But I tell you that anyone who looks at a woman with a lustful eye, has already committed adultery with her in his heart. 29. Therefore if your eye is giving you this kind of trouble, gouge it out and throw it away. It is better for you to lose a part of your body than to have your whole body go to hell. 30. The same applies to your hand.

If your right hand is responsible for your sinning, hack it off and fling it away, too. Again, it is better to lose a part of your body, than to have your whole body go into hell.

I TELL YOU. Jesus startled His listeners when He said ANGRY THOUGHTS directed toward another, broke the 6th commandment as surely as the ACT OF MURDER. And from that penetrating declaration flows a breath-taking truth which applies to all of God's commandments — WHEN GOD FORBIDS SOMETHING: HE FORBIDS ALL ELSE ASSOCIATED WITH IT. We'll see that principle applied to adultery. The Pharisees insisted the 7th commandment was not broken until the OUTWARD ACT was committed. But that's because they refused to see God's law as aimed at the heart. As the true Interpreter of the law, Jesus counters — "But I tell you . . . " simply looking at a woman with lust in your eye, is the same as being in bed with her. Inasmuch as God sees the heart (imagination), what occurs in the believer's mind as fantasy, is actually taking place in front of God.

God sees what is going on in your mind as though it were actually happening.

matt. 5

Jesus sees lustful thoughts

AS GOD SEES

The drawing focuses on the Pharisee error. Limiting the 7th commandment to an outward act, they ignored the principle that the commandment forbids everything else **associated with the act** — particularly that occurring in the heart (the imagination). Inasmuch as GOD IS SPIRIT, scenes in the mind ACTUALLY TAKE PLACE in His sight. Why? The imagination IS SPIRIT too. Remember: "God looks on the heart" (I Sam. 16:7). Therefore, whatever takes place in the imagination, is clearly done in the sight of God. For the believer committed to pleasing the Lord, the IMAGINATION is the place where he must work the hardest. The notion that what a person thinks is his own private business, is false. How come? "All things are open to the eyes of Him with Whom we have to do!" (Heb. 4:12,13).

COMMENT: In discussing adultery, it's important to state that SEX, in God's eyes, is far from dirty. It's a heavenly gift, meant to be exciting and fulfilling. To insist that sex is solely for having children, is nonsense. Were that so, God would have installed regulators in our bodies, as in the animals, so we'd have children in season. As it is, children are the BY-PRODUCT of sex. A man is to find pleasure in his mate and vice versa. God purposely made woman attractive to man, good to look upon. So when a man sees a woman that appeals to him, goes after her and wins her — and marries her — that's when the FUN BEGINS. That's when SEX BEGINS. God intends for it to END in marriage, too. That is, all the delights, thrills and pleasures of sex, belong INSIDE marriage. When it comes to SEX APART FROM MARRIAGE, that's what the 7th commandment is all about.

LUSTFUL EYE. It is clear the 7th commandment forbids, not just sex acts outside of marriage, but everything else associated with it. This applies as much as to how girls dress as to dirty jokes, books and movies. It's one thing to be ATTRACTIVE, another to be SEDUCTIVE, and girls know the difference. So do men. Anything that presents sexual stimulation to the eye or ear is forbidden. This means there should be NO LOOKING OR THINKING about sex apart from marriage. Once a person LOOKS and allows a fantasy to develop in his or her mind, that's when impurity begins. It's true that Satan can generate all sorts of tempting scenes in the imagination, but there is NO IMPURITY (no sin) until the believer latches onto a scene and indulges in it. Temptation is not sin (Heb. 4:15). Yielding to it — IS. Apparently there is NO RESTRAINT on sexual pleasure INSIDE THE MARRIAGE as long as the delights are mutual. God intends for the intimacy to be exciting and fulfilling, for in a mysterious way, it pictures the believer's completeness and satisfaction in Christ (Eph. 5:31,32).

matt. 5

JESUS' TEACHING VERSUS MODERN SOCIETY

PHARISEES	JESUS
Only the act breaks the law. Everything else is beyond the law.	The law forbids everything associated with sex outside of marriage.

The Pharisees would be popular today. What they did to God's law, modern society is trying to duplicate. Our permissive nation LAUGHS at the prohibition of sex outside of marriage. It works hard through movies, popular songs and talk shows to REMOVE ALL GUILT from sexual freedom. Jesus' words seem lost on a society that is doing everything possible to justify TOTAL SEXUAL FREEDOM. For those of us in the SCHOOL OF KINGS, however, there's no choice. If we want to please God, our hearts must be set on being like Christ. Then God, Who SEES OUR HEARTS, views not only our shame, but our DESIRE to be like Him. While we all fail badly in this area, we nonetheless rejoice . . . that with God: TRYING IS WINNING.

HAND/EYE. No one yawned when Jesus preached. His statements were so graphic listeners often lost their breath. They were stunned when He said, "If your eye causes you to sin, gouge it out and throw it away." And the same for the hand. He could have included the foot and ear, for it applies to them, too. He's not speaking literally, of course, for you can cut off all these parts and still be impure of heart — where God sees. EYES have to do with what you SEE. EARS with what you HEAR, FEET where you GO. and HANDS with what you DO. When your eyes meet a tempting sight, "DON'T LOOK AT IT," says Jesus. Act as though your eye had been cut out of your head. And if your ears meet stimulating words, "DON'T LISTEN!" Behave as though you HAD NO EARS. The same is true of hands and feet. Jesus is speaking of the RUTHLESSNESS with which we're to deal with this sin in our lives. He is NOT asking us to MUTILATE our bodies, but to MORTIFY (crucify) our sexual impulses (Col. 3:5). For the FEW MINUTES we have on earth, the Lord asks BEATITUDE MEN/WOMEN to deal ruthlessly with all sexual stimulation apart from marriage. It will be worth it, He says, "For at my right hand are pleasures forever more!" (Psa. 16:11). In other words, "It will be worth it all,. when we see Jesus!"

matt. 5

"If the law is so inclusive with regard to adultery, where does that put divorce?"

31. You've also been told that **"If a man wants to divorce his wife, he must give her the proper divorce certificate."** 32. But I tell you that anyone who divorces his wife, except for marital fraud, causes her to commit adultery if she marries again. And anyone who marries her commits adultery.

DIVORCE. Jesus said a lot more on divorce than we find in these verses. Matthew 19:3-10, gives a fuller picture of what was happening in Jesus' day and God's COMMAND regarding marriage.

matt. 5

According to Josephus, the Jewish historian, a man could divorce his wife FOR ANY REASON, as long as he was careful to give her the PROPER CERTIFICATE. The Pharisees focused on the piece of parchment given the woman, ignoring completely God's intention in marriage. Their "divorce paper" made a joke of marriage. A man could switch wives as often as he wished. Speaking squarely in the face of this licentious practice, Jesus announces the TRUE TEACHING on divorce. THERE IS NO PROVISION FOR DIVORCE, He says, as He reaffirms God's plan — ONE MAN AND ONE WOMAN for life — period. There is no exception. Why? The law represents the righteousness of God and there can be no exception to that. It is unthinkable that Jesus would insert an exception in the marriage law, after once given by God. "What God hath joined together," He insisted, "let no man separate" (Matt. 19:6).

Jesus insisted that God's original purpose for marriage was that one man and one woman be joined together as one as long as they both lived.

matt. 5

MARRIAGE— A MATTER OF THE HEART

The preacher hears their outward vows.

God sees their heart commitment.

We've learned that God's law applies to the HEART and is not limited to outward acts, as the Pharisees were teaching. A minister may say," I pronounce you man and wife," and the marriage is LEGAL in man's eyes. But God, seeing the hearts, beholds the actual love between two people. When a man takes a woman TO HIS HEART, God says, "You are now ONE FLESH, stay that way for the rest of your lives!" God allows us to CHOOSE our mates, but once that decision is made, we're stuck with the choice. He does not give us the privilege of changing our minds. That's why one must be careful in choosing a mate. Similarly, when hearts BECOME ESTRANGED, the couple is DIVORCED in God's sight, even though they continue to live under the same roof. It is the steadfast HEART UNION that God commands in marriage.

EXCEPT FOR: Though insisting He came to "fulfill the law," we find the Lord saying, "except for marital fraud." Is He actually making an exception to the marriage law? No. His exception has to do with a CUSTOM of those days. Marriages were often arranged by the families independantly of the couple. Many times it was not a "love match." Fortunes were sometimes involved and often a contract was signed. The man was **supposed** to be getting a virgin. If he didn't, the deal was off and the contract cancelled. To protect the girl's claim to virginity, the couple spent the first night on a sheet. The next day the girl displayed the sheet publicly. It may not sound too nice, but that sheet was important to the girl. She folded it and put it away as her "token of virginity." Later, if her husband claimed fraud, the sheet was brought out to prove her virginity. Jesus' exception PERTAINS TO THIS CUSTOM. He is saying in effect, "If the marriage should be called off because of fraud, by all means give the girl a certificate so that she won't be forced into prostitution." The exception has no application today.

COMMITS ADULTERY. The original marriage law, as re-affirmed by Jesus, stands with NO EXCEPTION. It is one man - one woman for life. But how do we, as imperfect people, fare under this perfect law? Not very well. We don't do any better with the marriage law than we do with any of the other commandments. The percentage of LEGAL DIVORCES among Christians is very high. The spiritual divorce rate is even higher. Behind the doors of their homes, many break the HEART-BOND (which God sees), yet continue to live together for a host of reasons (children, finances, convenience, etc). Still, it is adulterous as far as God is concerned. Even BEATITUDE-PEOPLE meet with failure in their marriages, but they have the TOOLS for success in God's eyes. Their poverty of spirit, meekness and peacemaker qualities aid them in working through most marital difficulties. For those working hard in the SCHOOL OF KINGS, divorce should be unthinkable. But failures do occur, even when you've done your best. In that case, it is fabulous to realize that with God: TRYING IS WINNING. When a believer TRIES HARD to make his marriage work, he is keeping the marriage law as far as God is concerned.

GOD'S PROVISION FOR MARITAL FAILURE

In setting a perfect standard before imperfect men, God knows failures will occur. If angry thoughts break the 6th commandment, and the lustful look breaks the 7th, then ESTRANGED HEARTS break the marriage law. Aware of man's failure under the law, God has provided a remedy — THE CROSS. This is why He TOLERATES separation, divorce, remarriage and the adulterous state. He hates it, but CALVARY COVERS IT ALL. Knowing God sees the heart, BEATITUDE-PEOPLE put **their hearts** into making their marriages work. Out of their deep commitment to Jesus, they try to live for their mates, rather than themselves. To God, that is fulfilling the LAW OF MARRIAGE. Should a marriage fail after a believer has done his best, he is still a success in God's eyes!

matt. 5

"Inasmuch as the Pharisees were swearing by the temple and the altar, what should beatitude people do about using an oath to back up their word?"

33. What's more, you've heard that long ago the people were told, **"Do not break your oath,"** and **"give the Lord what you swear to give Him."** 34. But I tell you, do not swear at all — not by heaven, for it is God's throne; 35. nor by earth, for it is His footstool; nor by Jerusalem, for it is the city of the Great King. 36. And do not swear by your head, for you cannot make one hair, white or black. 37. When you speak, let your "yes" mean "yes," and your "no," mean, "no." Anything you say beyond that will be from the devil.

6th Commandment

"DON'T KILL"

Angry thoughts
Looks
Words

JESUS' TEACHING WIDENS THE LAW'S APPLICATION

Watching the Lord give the TRUE INTERPRETATION of the law, we behold a great principle — WHENEVER GOD FORBIDS SOMETHING, HE FORBIDS ALL ELSE ASSOCIATED WITH IT. In the circle above, I've placed the 6th commandment — "Thou shalt not commit murder." While the Pharisees limited that commandment to the ACT of taking a life, the Lord told us that same commandment applies to ANGRY THOUGHTS, ANGRY LOOKS, ANGRY WORDS. I have drawn a LARGE CIRCLE around the commandment to show the wider application. We saw the same thing with regard to ADULTERY. Will this also be true as the Lord moves to other matters of the law? We'll see.

matt. 5

OATHS. When Jesus speaks of oaths, He's not referring to profanity, but the practice of USING SOMETHING SOLEMN to make people believe what you say is true. You've heard them: "I swear on my mother's grave . . . I swear on a stack of Bibles . . I swear by all that's holy!" The reason for this? Men are such LIARS, their word cannot be taken at face value. This is why we have ESCROW OFFICES. Because one man's word cannot be trusted by another, it has to be reinforced some way. Use of the OATH goes back to Old Testament times. Thus we find Moses providing for the OATH when people made promises to God (Num. 30:2; Deut. 23:21-24). In fact, God used an oath to back His word to Abraham (Heb. 6:17). God's Word is sufficient of course, but for Abraham's sake, a man accustomed to the oath, God did it that the partiarch might view God's promise as unbreakable.

NOT BY HEAVEN. In Jesus' day, the Pharisees were playing games with the oath. Instead of using it to establish TRUTHFULNESS (it's real purpose), they developed LEGAL WAYS in which the oath could be used to DECEIVE. An entire section of the Jewish legal code (the Mishnah), was devoted to WHEN an oath was binding and when it was not. When the oath included GOD'S NAME, they had to keep it. So they began to swear by things RELATED TO GOD, thus avoiding the use of His name. If a man swore by Jerusalem, for example, he was NOT BOUND. But if he swore TOWARD Jerusalem, he had to keep his word. By such ARTIFICIAL MEANS, the oath was no longer a basis for truth, but could be used to reinforce A LIE. The Lord was addressing this practice when He said, "Don't swear by heaven, for it is God's throne, etc. . . " In other words, no matter what the Pharisees used, whether temple or altar, they were still swearing by God. There is no such thing as a trivial oath, says Jesus. Every oath is a solemn pledge to tell the truth.

matt. 5

BUT I TELL YOU. To His disciples, the Lord said, "DON'T SWEAR AT ALL!" Beatitude-people don't need oaths. If the purpose behind the oath is TRUTHFULNESS, and the Lord's people are committed to truthfulness, then they don't need to swear by anything. They are people of the truth, following a man (Christ Jesus) Who is **the truth** (John 14:6). The Lord says, "I want your 'yes' to mean 'yes' — no double talk, no hidden meanings. Say what you mean, mean what you say." The Christian who goes beyond this, seeking to be clever or subtle, steps into SATAN'S territory. Since we all have OLD NATURES THAT LOVE TO LIE, Satan can get lies out of our mouths easily — if we make any attempt to deceive. After all, he's the FATHER OF LIES (John 8:44). The moment we start to say anything but the truth, he can bring words to our lips. You know that when you're angry, what awful things roll from your lips. Similarly, when we go beyond the SIMPLE TRUTH, the devil will be behind the next words out of our mouths.

The Christian who wants to be clever or subtle can easily fall into the snare of letting lies inspired by Satan come out of his mouth. There is also the temptation to embellish an experience we are relating to others and including untruths in our conversation.

matt. 5

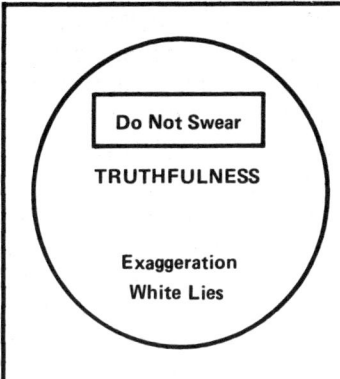

THE WIDE PRINCIPLE APPLIED TO THE USE OF THE OATH

- Do Not Swear
- TRUTHFULNESS
- Exaggeration
- White Lies

Behind the use of the oath is TRUTHFULNESS. The large circle pictures Jesus' broader application of His words — "Don't swear at all." When believers relate personal experiences, the temptation is to EXAGGERATE. Satan, knowing we like to make events exciting and vivid, is ready to help us say more than the facts allow. It is very HUMAN to want to impress people; it is very NATURAL to try and make ourselves look good; it is also very SATANIC. White lies, the keeping of promises to pray for someone, even being on time, all come under Jesus' wider application of DON'T SWEAR. We shouldn't even let people BELIEVE EXAGGERATED things about us. Think of that the next time you hear a guest speaker being introduced. Truthfulness is to pervade every area of our lives.

"When a beatitude man is abused, does he have any right to strike back at all?"

38. You have heard that long ago Moses told the people, **"If one man puts out another man's eye, he must pay for it with his own eye. And if he knocks out another man's tooth, one of his own teeth must be knocked out."** 39. But I tell you, do not resist the man who does evil to you. For example, if someone should strike you on the right cheek,

matt. 5

offer him your left cheek as well. 40. If a soldier asks you to carry his luggage for a mile, do it for two miles. 42. If a beggar asks for your money, give it. And if anyone wants to borrow from you, don't turn your back on him.

EYE/TOOTH. When people set about to AVENGE THEMSELVES against others, they usually go overboard. Intense feelings lead them to go beyond what's fair or just. This is why God established the RETALIATION LAW for ancient Israel. In Exodus 21:22, God says through Moses, "When two men are fighting . . . and anyone is injured, you shall give life for life, eye for eye, tooth for tooth, hand for hand . . . etc." Please note, however, this famous law was given to JUDGES AND MAGISTRATES. It was for the COURTS. The purpose was to make sure that punishment fitted the crime and did not go further than that. But the Pharisees, as we have seen them twist other laws, extended this one to INDIVIDUALS. They took it out of the courts **where it belonged,** and placed it in the hands of men **where it did not belong.** Thus they taught a man COULD AVENGE HIMSELF **personally** against his neighbor. So when Jesus says, "BUT I SAY UNTO YOU . . . ," He is not denouncing the law, but the practice of the Pharisees/doctors in making it **personal.**

DON'T RESIST. It is not surprising that Jesus would teach His disciples NON-RESISTANCE. As BEATITUDE-PEOPLE, they're expected to be merciful and peacemakers. They don't deal with wrongs — they forgive. It's God's business to handle wrongs. He does it on earth through governments and courts. In heaven, He'll deal with anything that hasn't been cared for on earth at the final judgment . . . all accounts will be balanced out — in the last day. Knowing this, the BEATITUDE MAN relaxes. No matter what ABUSE he suffers, whether loss of money, time, possessions, or even personal injury — he doesn't retaliate. He knows God will equalize everything in time. He doesn't allow a vengeful spirit to arise within him. He doesn't even get upset. How come? He knows ABUSES are normal for those in the SCHOOL OF KINGS. When you're taking a course in BEING LIKE JESUS, you can expect abuse. He took abuse — all the way to Calvary. So He's not asking us to do something He hasn't done. Until we suffer abuse, an important part of our schooling is missing.

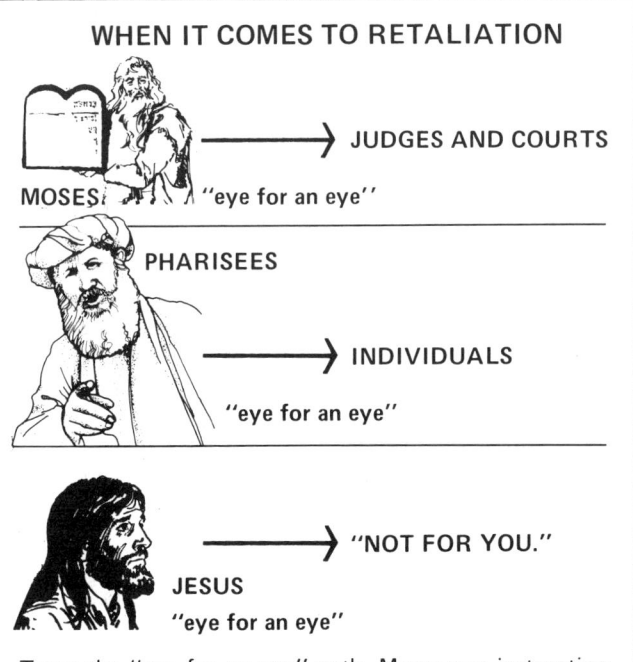

WHEN IT COMES TO RETALIATION

MOSES ⟶ JUDGES AND COURTS
"eye for an eye"

PHARISEES ⟶ INDIVIDUALS
"eye for an eye"

JESUS ⟶ "NOT FOR YOU."
"eye for an eye"

Trace the "eye for an eye" path. Moses was instructing the judges in Israel. But the Pharisees extended the law to individuals. The Lord said that law is not for you. You live by another law, the law of love. You love people no matter what they do to you. You follow My example: do not retaliate. Don't resist. Don't even get upset. Instead, do as your Father in heaven does — do them good.

matt. 5

97

matt. 5

FOR EXAMPLE. The Lord takes four examples from Jewish life to show how far BEATITUDE PEOPLE should carry their **non-retaliation**. In each case evil is being done to you: 1.) striking you on the face, 2.) taking you to court, 3.) commandeering your service, 4.) begging you for money. Yet, in the face of these abuses, you are so in control of your own spirit, and love others so powerfully, you reject any thought of retaliation. Even when your rights are violated, you don't let it irritate you. You gladly go the SECOND MILE with a smile on your face, knowing such an attitude is a SHOCK to your abuser. It's a DYNAMITE WITNESS. Knowing that God is watching and will more than compensate you in that day, makes it possible for you to GIVE UP YOUR RIGHTS, CHEERFULLY. It really costs you nothing — in the long run. In the meantime you are CHANGING into the likeness of the Lord, acting more and more like Him. Though you may think it is costing you something NOW, you are truly thrilling the heart of God. You can't lose doing that.

By willingly suffering abuse without retaliating, we walk in the Lord's steps.

AWARE OF GOD'S EYES

matt. 5

As we progress through the SCHOOL OF KINGS, we learn there are NO ACCIDENTS in the life of a Christian. Everything that happens, whether a blow to the face or people suing us, is a part of God's plan. He controls the timing. He arranges the circumstances. He watches our hearts, noting our REACTION to each situation He allows to come against us. The more we become aware of God's eyes, the less we care that our rights are abused. In fact, we find it possible to act as though we had NO RIGHTS: no right to retaliate, no right to cling to possessions, time or money. His pleasure soars when He sees us taking abuse and acting as HE WOULD. Again, I must say we are talking about the perfect standard. Even though imperfect Christians cannot attain to such a high standard — THEY CAN ALWAYS TRY. You already know how God feels about our TRYING.

matt. 5

100

COMMENT: Reading through this passage for the first time, one might ask, "**Are we supposed to take it no matter what anyone does or says to us? Doesn't that make us doormats?**" No. There are 3 ways to respond to abuse: PASSIVELY — AGGRESSIVELY — ASSERTIVELY. PASSIVE BEHAVIOR is when we give no outward response of any kind, regardless of how much we're hurt or humiliated. AGGRESSIVE BEHAVIOR is when we allow anger to surge within us to the point where we retaliate with words or actions that strike back. ASSERTIVE BEHAVIOR is healthy and proper and can be done in a way that fits God's plan. The apostle Paul was assertive when he insisted on being tried at Rome (Acts 25:10,11). Jesus was assertive when He was arrested and questioned by the high priest. "Why ask Me?" He said, "ask those who heard Me" (John 18:21). That wasn't passive. No matter how helpless the situation may seem, there's one way we can always ASSERT OURSELVES — by doing MORE THAN IS ASKED OF US.

When Jesus was brought before the high priest, he acted in an assertive manner. There are times when we too will find it necessary to be assertive in our dealings with those who abuse us.

DOING MORE THAN IS ASKED OF US

matt. 5

Note the examples Jesus gives: turning the other cheek, giving the coat and going the second mile. In each case we're to DO MORE THAN ASKED OF US. No one commands us to do it, we do it as an ASSERTIVE ACTION **by our own free choice**. It is a right we can never lose. When believers GO BEYOND what is asked, it is a POWERFUL STATEMENT, a dynamic witness. But only a BEATITUDE CHRISTIAN in the school of kings can do it. It takes a person who knows God is watching him closely and will recompense him for any loss. But it does something else for the Christian — it PUTS HIM IN CONTROL. No longer is he the helpless victim. He feels great about himself as he ACTS LIKE GOD. This makes for good emotional and mental health, even in the face of the worst situation. As the days become more evil and Christians are fiercely abused, it will be very wise to meet the situation with ASSERTIVE BEHAVIOR such as Jesus teaches us here.

matt. 5

"Whew! That's pretty high ground! Have we reached the climax of Jesus' teaching, or is there still higher ground before us?"

43. You have heard it said, **"Love your neighbor and hate your enemy."** 44. But I say to you: love your enemies! Pray for those persecuting you! 45. In doing this, you will prove you are the true sons of your Father in heaven. For He makes His sun to rise on the evil and the good and sends rain on the just and the unjust. 46. If you love only those who love you, what reward can you expect for that? Even the tax-gougers show that kind of love. 47. And if you give a friendly greeting only to your brothers, in what way are you different from anyone else? Even the hated Gentiles do that. 48. No, my friends, you're to be perfect, even as your Father in heaven is perfect.

LOVE YOUR NEIGHBOR. The rabbis were teaching the people to love their neighbors, but hate their enemies. Where would they get such an idea? They arrived at it by playing games with the Scriptures. When they came upon a passage that seemingly imposed impossible demands on them, they looked for loopholes in the law. In this case, they took the passage in Leviticus 19, which says, "DO NOT SEEK REVENGE AGAINST ANY OF YOUR PEOPLE, BUT LOVE YOUR NEIGHBOR AS YOURSELF" (vs.18). Since God was addressing the congregation of Israel, they reasoned, our neighbors have to be our **fellow Jews.** Our neighbors consist of family and friends within the Jewish community — therefore all the rest are OUTSIDERS. Inasmuch as we're to love our own, it follows we MUST HATE OUTSIDERS. That was their LOOPHOLE, a scriptural twist. The Scriptures, of course never hinted such a thing. So when Jesus appeared on the scene as the TRUE INTERPRETER of the law, they finally learned who their neighbor really was.

LOVE YOUR ENEMIES. If we thought refusing to resist anyone doing evil to us was high ground, we have HIGHER GROUND before us now. We have come to the HIGHEST POINT, the greatest challenge of the Sermon on the Mount — LOVING OUR ENEMIES! Those listening to Jesus must have been stunned to hear that "NEIGHBOR" included ENEMIES as well as friends. When He says LOVE THEM, He means: speak kindly to those persecuting you in a tender, loving voice that shows no hint of hostility. Do them good, even if you have to sacrifice to do it. And pray for them even as they're abusing you. Now that's some standard. Imagine asking God to forgive someone persecuting you, with no hostility in your voice. Who can do such a thing? Your heavenly Father does it all the time, says Jesus, and you can too. When you do, you prove you're His sons, because no one else in the world can act like that. This kind of love is SUPER LOVE — absolutely supernatural!

matt. 5

The highest point in the Sermon on The Mount is the teaching of our Lord on loving our enemies . . . those who have treated us cruelly and have abused us. By speaking kindly to them and showing love to them, we please God very much and open a way whereby our persecutors may have a desire implanted within them to trust Christ.

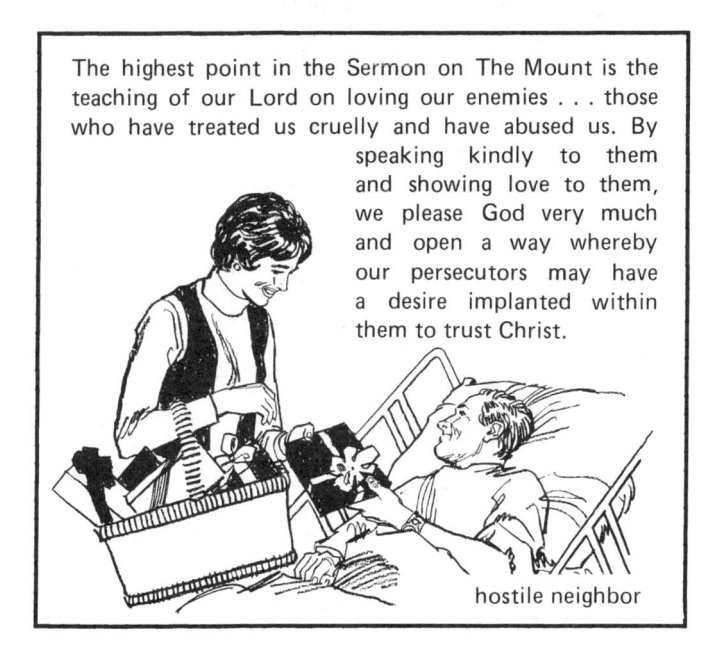

hostile neighbor

matt. 5

SUPER LOVE

As the spikes were being driven into Jesus' hands, He no doubt whispered, "Father forgive them." Now that is SUPER LOVE, exceeding anything known to man. Human love: love for parents and children and mates and friends is wonderful. Even the worst of scoundrels, says Jesus, exhibit this kind of love for each other. But to LOVE AN ENEMY goes far beyond anything human. Even so, BEATITUDE-PEOPLE can show this kind of love. Jesus is not asking the impossible. Born of God, true believers possess the DIVINE NATURE (II Pet. 1:4). Given the supernatural ability of the Holy Spirit, they are **capable of** PERFECT LOVE, divine love. Because you are the sons of your Father in heaven, commands the Lord, you should display this love and let the world see the DIFFERENCE. It is your DIFFERENCE that counts with God. It is this difference, He uses to condemn the world.

PERFECT AS GOD? Can believers be as perfect as God? Yes, at times. In those moments when he/she is completely yielded to the Holy Spirit, the DIVINE NATURE, God's own nature, is manifested in the Christian's life. In such a moment, the believer can **supernaturally** love an enemy — something impossible for natural man. For as long as the Christian's surrender persisits, he will behave like God, manifesting the perfection of God. And for that brief interval, he will be as perfect as God. What the Lord's sermon is asking for, is MORE AND MORE of those moments in TOUGHER AND TOUGHER situations. This of course, is what the **school of kings** is all about — changing us more and more into the likeness of God. The more we display HIS PERFECTION, the better we're doing in the school of kings.

matt. 5

105

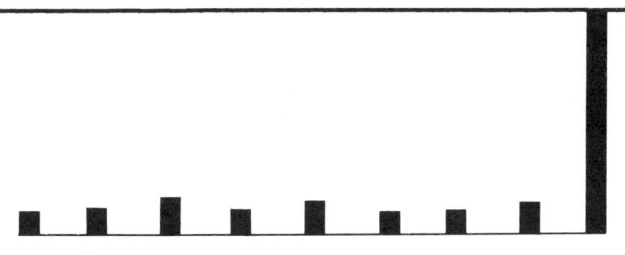

See that big vertical line running off the chart? That represents God's perfection. See the tiny vertical lines alongside His? They represent the times we display HIS PERFECTION. We'll never match His perfection in this life, but the thing to see is it is the SAME PERFECTION. The difference is **IN DEGREE,** not in **kind.** When Jesus says we're to be perfect as God is perfect, He's not saying we're to MATCH HIS LINE, i.e., be perfect all the time — we can't. The FIGHT against the flesh is so awesome we can't come close to matching His perfection. Ah, but we can try. The Lord asks us to TRY and make our line go as high as we can. The higher we GO, the more our lives GLOW with the supernatural. The more we GLOW, the more we are LIKE HIM,

matt. 5

SUMMARY

NOT HAPPINESS, BUT HOLINESS

Bear in mind our one purpose for being on this earth — preparing for the next life. The Lord didn't put us here to settle down and be comfortable. We're here for one reason only — to become like Jesus (Rom. 8:29). God is getting us ready for a life with Him. He is producing companions for eternity, considering our time on earth as a **school for kings.** Therefore the GOAL of the Christian life is **not happiness,** BUT HOLINESS. Don't let that statement sail over your head. Let it seize you. You'll never be the same. This is what the Sermon on the Mount is all about — forsaking the ways of the world; ignoring its offers and believing we'll never be sorry if we use this one life to become like the Lord.

matt. 5

A GRAPHIC VIEW OF CHAPTER FIVE

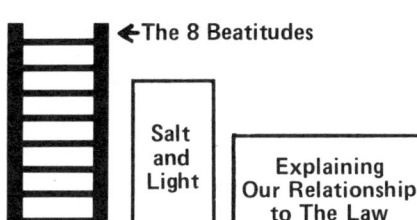

← The 8 Beatitudes

Salt and Light

Explaining Our Relationship to The Law

6 Items of The Law Explained by Jesus

You've seen this drawing before. It's a visual overview of chapter five. Now that we've completed the chapter, we can look at the chart again and observe the Lord's FORMAT for communicating the truths. What He is saying is this: Blessed is the man who is LIKE GOD, and then breaks godliness down into 8 beatitudes so that we can examine it piece by piece. After telling us to be SALT & LIGHT and explaining our relationship to the LAW, He asks 6 things of us that are contrary to the ways of the world. He outlaws ANGER, the LOOK OF LUST, WHITE LIES, and RETALIATION. He asks us to GO BEYOND the natural and RETURN GOOD FOR EVIL. Finally, He asks us to do something that is really impossible for natural man — LOVE OUR ENEMIES! He sums it all by saying: "BE PERFECT," because your heavenly Father is perfect. What could be clearer? He wants more than good works from us — HE WANTS US TO BE LIKE GOD!

Because Christ died for us and rose again from the dead, we have the same resurrection power working within us. Therefore the Christian life is one of Christ living through us. It is because of this that we can become progressively more like our Lord.

matt. 6

"Now that the Lord has explained what we're to BE — like our heavenly Father; will He go on and tell us HOW He wants us to live out any perfection we acquire?"

6 1. Beware of doing your good deeds publicly, simply to be seen of men. If you do, you forfeit any reward your Father in heaven might have for you. 2. Therefore, when you're about to give alms to the needy, don't announce it as the hypocrites do, blowing trumpets in the synagogues and in the streets. Hungry for the praise of men, they do this to draw attention to their deeds of charity. I assure you, they've received in full all the reward they'll ever get. 3. So when you embark on an act of kindness, do it for God's eyes alone. Do it so secretly, that your left hand doesn't know what your right hand is doing. 4. Then your Father, who sees everything done in secret, will reward you.

> Our giving is to be for the eyes of Christ alone, not to be seen by men to receive their praise, otherwise we wipe out any reward God might have for us.

SEEN OF MEN. With this chapter comes a shift in the Lord's teaching. In chapter 5, He set forth the kind of people His disciples are to BE. After explaining the BE-attitudes and commenting on the law, He concluded by saying, "You are to be perfect as your Father in heaven is perfect." Now He tells us to BEWARE how we go about displaying our likeness to our heavenly Father, making sure we don't do it to be SEEN OF MEN. If we do it to obtain HUMAN PRAISE, He warns, we wipe out any reward God might have for us. This is most tricky, since our choice lies between pleasing God, WHOM WE CANNOT SEE, and men WHOM WE CAN SEE. Our choice is influenced by the fact that we have an OLD NATURE that loves praise and recognition. But there's no way, says Jesus, you can do good works for the praise of people and still expect God to reward you.

THE PROBLEM AREA FOR CHRISTIANS
UNTO GOD → **BEFORE OTHERS**

Called to live a life UNTO GOD, believers have to live that life BEFORE MEN. With the human heart "desperately wicked and deceitful above all things," this is tricky business (Jer. 17:9). The devil knows all about our EGOS and how much the OLD NATURE craves praise and recognition. So he puts pressure on us to seek the approval of men, rather than God. He suggests that praise from an UNSEEN GOD is nowhere near as satisfying as praise from **flesh and blood** men. The more carnal we are, the more we heed Satan's suggestion. The more mature we are, the more we resist the devil's suggestion and do our good deeds for God's eyes alone.

matt. 6

GOOD DEEDS. The Lord will cite THREE SPECIFIC AREAS in which His beatitude people must exercise caution: 1.) **alms-giving** (vss. 2-4); 2.) **praying** (vss. 5-14); 3.) **fasting** (vss. 16-18). Alms-giving is mentioned first, probably because it held such an important place in Jewish life. Performing deeds of mercy to the poor and unfortunate, was deeply ingrained in the Jews. Because He is generous, God expects His people to be generous. However, He is not so concerned with the ACT of giving as with HOW the gift is given. That is, He cares more what the HEART is doing, than what the HAND is doing. Since "God looks on the heart," rather than the outward appearance, His eyes are focused on the believer's heart to see if his ATTITUDE is right. THREE ATTITUDES are possible in the act of giving.

PRAISE OF MEN   PRAISE OF SELF   PRAISE OF GOD

THREE ATTITUDES OF THE HEART

Definitely outlawed is giving for the eyes of men, **to gain their praise.** This was a huge sin of the Pharisees, whom Jesus here calls — HYPOCRITES. He visualizes them on their way to put money in the poor box, with an entourage of trumpeteers heralding their way to the temple. The action may be overdescribed, but it accurately pictures what was in their hearts. Another attitude is that of the Christian who **praises himself** for his deeds. His actions may be **done in secret,** yet in his heart he is congratulating himself for being so generous and pious. Although it is all done IN SECRET, it is sufficient to WIPE OUT any reward the believer might have earned from God. Giving to please the Lord is the ONLY ATTITUDE that earns a reward, for there is no difference between secret pride and open pride, as far as God is concerned. Pleasing the Lord must be the Christian's ONLY motive for giving.

SECRET. We're not to take Jesus' words so precisely that we close our eyes when we make out our checks. That's not what He means. Some Christians won't use checks or keep track of their giving, just for secrecy's sake. But that's not what the Lord is after. It's not the secrecy that is important, but the heart that **doesn't want** the praise of men: a heart that will HIDE **from men and self,** in order to seek praise from God alone. When He says the LEFT HAND is not to know what the RIGHT HAND is doing, He means the NEW MAN is to do the giving in such a way that the OLD MAN has no part in it. How is that done? By giving in the spirit. That means, planning your gift with the Lord, talking to Him as you present it, and FORGETTING it once it has been made. The believer must be content to have God as THE ONLY WITNESS of his giving. Only in this way can PRAISE OF SELF be avoided.

REWARDS. Some Christians resent the idea of being rewarded by God for their giving. They'd rather give out of gratitude, they say, expecting nothing in return. That may sound pious, but it is dangerously risky. Man is so constituted that he NEEDS both rewards and praise. If he doesn't get them from God, he'll get them from another source. But get them he will, and from sources subtle and hard to detect. That's the risk. God knows He made man with this need and that's why He made rewards PART OF HIS PROGRAM, rewards so enticing Moses was willing to abandon the wealth of Egypt for them (Heb. 11:26). It is dangerous NOT TO SEEK God's praise, for the OLD NATURE will see that you get it one way or another. Settling for MAN'S PRAISE or YOUR OWN is a bad trade, for neither really satisfies. God's praise, on the other hand, lasts forever. Let God say to you, "I'M

matt. 6

matt. 6

PROUD OF YOU! YOU'VE DONE WELL!" and the pleasure and satisfaction that brings will remain with you throughout eternity. Why? God's delight in you is PERMANENT, for He never changes (Heb. 13:8).

"What about the Lord's second illustration of doing things for God's eyes alone?"

5. This brings us to the matter of prayer. When you pray, don't be like the hypocrites who love to stand in the synagogues and on the street corners, parading their prayers before men. They want everyone to see their piety and admire them. I assure you, this human praise is all the reward they'll ever get.

HYPOCRITES. Having brought up the matter of prayer, the Lord continues to refer to the Pharisees as hypocrites. Even in this, their hearts prefer the praise of men to the praise of God. In Jesus' day, all devout Jews stopped what they were doing and prayed when the trumpet sounded for the morning sacrifice, the midday sacrifice and the evening sacrifice. If they were seated in a synagogue, they rose to their feet. If they were on a street corner, they stood right where they were and prayed. This was the custom. But the Pharisees did it with such ostentation, everyone had to notice them. They lifted their hands toward heaven, reciting Psalms or Old Testament prayers with great displays of feeling. Out of the corners of their eyes, they scanned to see if people were looking. They were not praying to God, but to BE SEEN AND HEARD OF MEN. There is no way they can expect any answers from God, says Jesus. They wanted praises from men and that's what they got — as their only reward.

6. So when you pray, get off by yourself. Go into your secret place and shut yourself up in the presence of God, out of the sight of men. Then your unseen

Father, who meets with you in the secret place, will reward you. 7. But when you do this, don't go on and on, babbling meaningless phrases like the pagans do. They think they're going to be heard for the sheer volume of their words. 8. You must not be like them. Actually, there's no need to carry on like that, for your Father knows full well what you need even before you ask.

matt. 6

> Jesus' teaching on prayer was revolutionary. No one had ever taught the things that He taught before.

WHEN YOU PRAY. These instructions were brand new to Jesus' disciples. **Secret praying** was just the opposite of the Jewish custom. So was His mention of the SECRET PLACE. Some translations use the word "closet." But the Greek word used here is, "tameion," a storeroom of sorts where one might keep his treasures. What Jesus is really referring to, is that ROOM IN OUR IMAGINATIONS where we behold the Lord when we close our eyes to pray. Everyone has such a room, for the imagination is the SANCTUARY of the soul. This is the ONLY PLACE where true worship can be offered to God. But it's not for worship only — it's also a place of fellowship. Here's where the Christian and his Lord meet to talk and enjoy each other. The imagination is spirit. Thoughts are spirit. And so is God. Later on when Jesus speaks to the "woman at the well," He will reveal this BIG TRUTH to her (John 4:24). Here the Lord is asking us to close our eyes — shut out the world — and visualize Him as being right there with us. The highest purpose of the imagination is not to plan space flights, but to give reality to the unseen Lord. Spending time with Jesus in the secret place — talking with Him spirit-to-spirit — is REAL PRAYING. The kind He seeks.

matt. 6

> **HOW WE VIEW JESUS**   **OUR SIDE**
> mirror/imagination screen
>
> **OUR IMAGE OF JESUS**
>
> When we visualize Jesus, we are projecting an image of Him on the SCREEN OF OUR MINDS. It's akin to watching TV. When we watch television, we don't actually see the person, but an image of him. And so with the Lord. We have no DIRECT CONTACT with Him, that would violate the faith-method. However, knowing **by faith** that He dwells within us, we can, **by faith,** project an image of Him on the imagination screen. We can legitimately visualize Him as being in the SECRET PLACE with us (Psa. 91:1).

MEETS WITH YOU. The Lord enjoys public praying, too . . . but it is vital that BEATITUDE MEN/WOMEN FIRST LEARN to enjoy Him in spirit-to-spirit fellowship. Not until they know Him INTIMATELY, will they develop a HUNGER FOR HIM, longing for Him during the day. Gradually they learn to MINISTER TO HIM, which is one of the great privileges of the faith-life. When we enter the secret place just to comfort Him and share ourselves with Him, we are on far higher ground than simply coming to ASK FOR THINGS. Consequently there is a BIG DIFFERENCE between **saying prayers and praying.** The Sermon on the Mount is teaching us the difference. Therefore, when we pray in public, it should be an extension of our private times with Jesus. Whether we pray publicly or privately, God is not so concerned with what the MOUTH is saying, as with what the HEART is saying. Our public praying will be much like our private times, once we learn to become INTIMATE with Jesus in the secret place.

BABBLING. The Lord cautions His disciples against stupidity in prayer. Inasmuch as God is a Father who loves His children, and already knows their needs, to recite endless strings of meaningless phrases is **ridiculous.** For Christians to resort to mechanical buildups of emotional fervor, is nonsense. It simply means they have not yet discovered the INTIMACY OF THE SECRET PLACE and have fallen into the practice of using clichés and crescendos to try and wrest blessings from God. God is not impressed with cultivated fervency. His disciples, who were with Him for 3 years, never talked to Him as we hear some do today. If God could be impressed by emotional babbling and worked up eloquence what kind of a person would that make Him? When you do this, says Jesus, you're acting like the hypocrites. So don't do it, He warns. You don't have that kind of a Father. You don't have to carry on in front of Him; neither can He be manipulated by THE ENERGY OF OUR PRAYER. Since He ALREADY KNOWS what we need and is eager to give it, it's totally unnecessary, even stupid.

FATHER KNOWS. Prayer goes far beyond asking things of God. Praying only to GET THINGS out of Him, reduces prayer to the level of begging. True prayer has to do with SHARING OURSELVES WITH HIM, showering our love and affection on Him. While God likes to be asked, He mostly aches for us to COME AND BE WITH HIM. That's what He died for — companionship and fellowship. It's **lonely at the top,** as one of our presidents used to say. And when people come only to GET and not to GIVE, it is even more lonely. The Lord hungers for those who care about His feelings and needs. Knowing it is lonely for Him at

matt. 6

times, they go out of their way to share themselves with Him. They may have to take time from something else, but they'll never be sorry for any love and affection they LAVISH on God. Some, reading Jesus' words, might be tempted to ask . . . **If God already knows our needs, why pray?** Now you know the answer. He needs us as much as we need Him. In prayer we have the exciting privilege of meeting God's needs as well as having our own met.

9. Then, when you start to pray, say something like this:

Our Father in heaven,
we hallow Your name,
10. May Your kingdom come,
may Your will be done on earth,
just as it is in heaven.

11. Give us today our daily bread,
12. and forgive us our sins, as we
have also forgiven those who sin
against us.*
13. Please don't allow us to be so
tempted, that we're overcome by the
evil one, but help us to overcome him.

START TO PRAY. Jesus' disciples were stunned, absolutely floored when Jesus said, "Our Father." It was total shock for them to think of God AS A PERSON — just like themselves. The Old Testament scarcely hints that God is a person. The image

---

*Some manuscripts add, "for yours is the kingdom and the power and the glory forever. Amen." When included, they testify to God's power to deliver. Elsewhere, it is stated that God will not allow us to be tempted beyond our ability to withstand. Clearly He is in control of all temptation.

(ICor. 10:13)

in most Jewish minds was that of a CLOUD BY DAY AND A PILLAR OF FIRE BY NIGHT. Yes, David knew Him as a person, but most viewed Him as a MIGHTY PRESENCE far removed from man. Our God is not like that, said Jesus. He's a person, a loving, caring Father Who wants us to talk to Him. For the disciples to think of themselves in GOD'S IMMEDIATE PRESENCE was a mind-blower. They had no idea how to act or what to say to Him. Sensing His disciples need for help in talking to God, the Lord gives them a model prayer. He doesn't mean for it to be a word for word exercise they would use over and over, but simply a guide to make it easier for them to START TALKING TO GOD. It is not to be repeated again and again, like the "HAIL MARYS" of the Roman church.

THE MODEL PRAYER AT A GLANCE

GOD'S AFFAIRS	OUR AFFAIRS
God's name	Give us
God's kingdom	Forgive us
God's will	Help us

Observe that God's affairs are first, then come ours. That's the proper order (Matt. 6:33). A person starts off, says Jesus, by hallowing or praising God's name. Actually, God has NO NAME, as we know names. He is not George Oscar Davis (G. O. D.), for in biblical terms, one's NAME is his CHARACTER. Jesus suggests His disciples begin their conversation praising God for what a fabulous PERSON He is, i. e., holy and true, faithful and just, merciful and kind, gentle and generous, patient and longsuffering, impartial and changeless, etc. After praising Him, they could express their longing for Jesus to return and take over the world, ruling it personally. In that day, God's will will be the rule of the land and enforced with a "rod of iron" (Rev. 2:27). For those who love righteousness, this will be a glorious event.

"How about our affairs?"

GIVE US. One should not think of "daily bread" solely in terms of food. Actually, this is a request that God provide what is needed to survive — day by day. Food is involved, but so is health, a home, a wife and children, a job and even a car, if one is needed for survival. However, when we ask God for daily bread, we should understand that God uses HUMAN MEANS of production and distribution to supply our needs. Nothing is lowered directly from the sky. Though a man gives thanks for the food in front of him, he still must work for it. As one says "GIVE US," he is reminded of his DAILY DEPENDENCE on the Lord, for even his job and all else that contributes to his welfare is from God. While salvation is free, inasmuch as it is priceless, everything else a believer gets he must EARN. Nothing is handed to anyone (2Thess. 3:10).

FORGIVE US. Daily forgiveness is as necessary to the health of the **soul**, as daily bread is for the health of the **body**. Our second request, therefore, is for the forgiveness of each day's sins. As it is impossible to drive across a city without breaking some traffic law, so is it impossible to go through a single day without offending God in some way. These sins, **unless forgiven**, can come between us and God, disrupting our fellowship with Him. Until we ask His forgiveness, they remain. But there are times when we might say to God, "I'm sorry, please forgive me," and God will reply, **"I'm sorry, I can't."** That occurs when we're unwilling to forgive those who sin against us. Unforgiveness in our hearts, makes it impossible for God to forgive us. One would think, that in view of the AWESOME DEBT God has forgiven us, Christians would find it easy to forgive others. But alas, many carry grudges and allow unforgiveness to linger in their hearts. While their salvation is not threatened by this, their fellowship with God IS BROKEN, and remains so, until they get rid of their unforgiveness (see page 121).

HELP US. The King James version reads, "And lead us not into temptation," which seems unfortunate in view of James' words, ". . . God cannot be tempted with evil, neither tempteth He any man" (Ja. 1:13). But what God does do, is ALLOW Satan to tempt us. But even then, never "beyond what you are able" (I Cor. 10:13 NASB). Actually, this request has to do with the struggle of the Christian life, that terrible warfare between flesh and spirit (Gal. 5:17). We all need temptation and testing, for God will not allow UNTESTED MATERIAL in the eternal kingdom. There can be no testing without temptation. Therefore all of us are involved in a DAILY BATTLE against sin. So the third request is for DAILY HELP in overcoming the evil one. In some cases we may have to ask for this help on an HOURLY BASIS, or even more often than that. Thus the Lord has given His disciples a rather rough guide to prayer. At least they have some idea how to start their conversations with God.

14. If you forgive the sins of others when they sin against you, your heavenly Father will forgive you. 15. But if you refuse to forgive others, your Father will not forgive your sins either.

NOT FORGIVE. After giving His disciples a broad outline for prayer, He returns to the matter of forgiveness. He wants them to understand the effect an UNFORGIVING HEART has on God. It puts Him in a place where He can't do for His own child and that causes Him great pain. God loves His children and wants to help them, but His hands are tied when Christians come to Him with unforgiving hearts. Why does Jesus stress this? Because FELLOWSHIP is God's greatest hunger. That's what Jesus died for. Christianity is a fellowship (1st John 1:3). So when we refuse to forgive others, we damage our relationship with God. He can handle a jealous heart, a covetous one, a greedy and selfish heart, yes, even a murderous heart, but

matt. 6

120

NOT an unforgiving heart. In the light of what He's forgiven us, it's UNTHINKABLE TO HIM, that we wouldn't forgive others. No matter what they did to us, it would be a TRIFLE compared to what He's forgiven — even if they killed our children. The price tag for harboring unforgiveness is frightful! There's no use trying to talk to God in this condition — or worship Him. Certainly you cannot expect answers to prayer. If you're having difficulty forgiving someone, you'd better get over it — FAST. The offense against you cannot begin to compare to the damage you're doing to yourself through unforgiveness!

To understand the consequences of unforgiveness, one needs to know the difference between SIN and SINS. The Lord taught the difference to His disciples in the upper room the night He was betrayed, at the last supper. Taking a towel and basin, He washed their feet. Since they were familiar with the Roman baths, they get the point when He said . . . "He that is washed, need not save to wash his feet" (John 13:10). Here's the point: Jesus' death on the cross took care of the GUILT OF SIN. All guilt is totally removed from every Christian. Sin cannot send a child of God to hell, for it is GUILT that brings punishment. However, the believer still sins and when sins are NOT CONFESSED, they mar his FELLOWSHIP with God. This is why daily confession is so urgent. (1st John 1:7) Fellowhip with God is impossible when UNFORGIVEN sin lingers in the heart. And so when a believer refused to forgive — and God cannot forgive him — his fellowship with God is broken until he gets rid of his bitterness. Yet the moment he forgives his neighbor, fellowship with God is restored. GUILT HAS TO DO WITH SIN, which was cared for at Calvary, "once for all" (Heb. 9:26; 10:10). FELLOWSHIP has to do with SINS which are confessed and cleansed daily (1st John 1:9).

"Have we now come to the Lord's third illustration of doing things for God's eyes alone?"

16. The same thing is true when you fast. Don't go around with pained looks on your faces, like the hypocrites do. They mark up their faces in such a way that people can't help but think they're fasting. Let me say once more, this is the only reward they'll ever get. 17. When you fast, groom yourselves. Look as nice as possible, 18. so that no one will suspect you're fasting, except your unseen Father, Who dwells in the secret place. He beholds the motives of your heart, and will reward you.

FAST. Having covered the matters of giving and praying, the Lord cites fasting as His third illustration of what He means by doing our DEEDS OF RIGHTEOUSNESS for God's eyes alone. This is startling to us, for fasting is a matter totally ignored today. As we listen to the Lord, it's clear He not only expects His disciples to fast, but even tells them HOW TO DO IT. Christian leaders today stress prayer and sacrificial giving, but who is stressing fasting? It's as though His words have been erased from the Bible. Yet the Word is full of it. You find it everywhere in the Old Testament and it clearly had its place in the early church (Acts 13:2 ff.). The early disciples, being Jews, grew up with fasting as a way of life. Even Jesus fasted 40 days and 40 nights (Matt. 4:2). It was part of Paul's ministry (Acts 14:23). The Lord clearly assumes fasting will have a place in the lives of His followers. His concern is not that His disciples would fast, but that WHEN they did it, it was not done for man's eyes, but for God's eyes alone.

HYPOCRITES. The Pharisees fasted often, or so they wanted the people to believe. Mondays and Thursdays were their regular days for fasting, plus all of the other fastings associated with the temple. They made quite a show of it, wearing pained expressions and using ashes to make their faces look pale. They wanted to appear DISMAL, DRAWN AND HAGGARD. That way people would observe them with pity and regard them as SUPER HOLY. Of course it was MANUFACTURED HOLINESS, for it appears they really didn't fast at all. They wore sackcloth about their heads so that no one could overlook their suffering. They wanted everyone to see what they were going through for their religion. Concerning them, the Lord says in effect, "They want people to admire them?, Fine. That's what they'll get. But that's ALL THEY'LL GET. They'll receive nothing from God. They now have their reward in full."

matt. 6

123

WHEN YOU FAST. Jesus instructs His disciples to keep their fasting to themselves. They are to avoid all OUTWARD appearances of fasting, considering GOD as their **only audience**. The Lord's earlier caution applies here also: if they fast for men's eyes, they WIPE OUT any reward they might have coming from God. The challenge is: why trade what God offers, for the FICKLE FAVOR of man? There are immediate rewards for fasting as well as future rewards. Whenever a person puts the Lord AHEAD OF FOOD (an astonishing event in our day), the pleasure it brings the Lord is tremendous. To forego eating for the purpose of SUBDUING THE FLESH and humbling yourself before God, brings all kinds of good things from God, both now and at the judgment. Fasting was the SECRET STRENGTH of the early church and when modern Christians rediscover the connection between prayer and fasting, a new power comes into their lives.

COMMENT: Fasting is not starving. These are separate matters, two different occurrences in the body. Each has a different chemistry. The body cannot starve until fasting has ended. God has placed an intelligence in the body that programs it to consume FATS, WASTES and TOXINS before any good tissue is consumed. The

matt. 6

average American could easily fast 20 to 30 days, because of the vast amount of STORED FUEL (fats and wastes) collected in the blood stream, organs and tissues. More fuel is stored OUTSIDE the body in the form of ROLLS OF FAT, usually around the middle. As long as a person has WATER TO DRINK, these stored fats, etc., are converted into a low grade fuel which will power the body nicely for days. Hunger normally vanishes after the first 48 hours, after which there is no more hunger until it is time to end the fast. The end of the fasting process is signaled by the RETURN OF HUNGER, at which time the body will begin to feed on itself — STARVATION. But there is NO STARVATION until the fats and wastes are consumed.

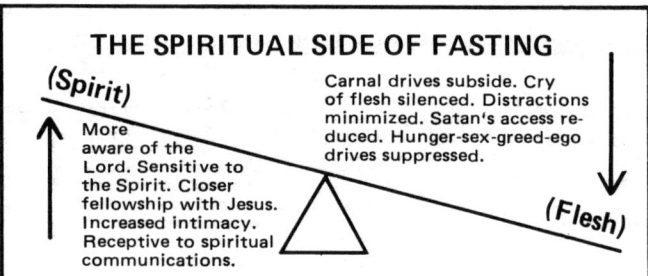

THE SPIRITUAL SIDE OF FASTING

(Spirit)
More aware of the Lord. Sensitive to the Spirit. Closer fellowship with Jesus. Increased intimacy. Receptive to spiritual communications.

Carnal drives subside. Cry of flesh silenced. Distractions minimized. Satan's access reduced. Hunger-sex-greed-ego drives suppressed.

(Flesh)

Around the 7th or 8th day of fasting the fleshly drives die down and spiritual sensitivity rises dramatically. The Lord becomes so real you can almost feel His arms about you. Intimacy is heightened and communication with Him is clearer. It is the ideal time for making a new commitment to Him as well as programming yourself for godly changes. On your first fast (or second) you may be too preoccupied with your body to notice the new spiritual awareness. But as you become used to fasting, you appreciate the NEW INTIMACY AND CONCENTRATION you enjoy with the Lord. In those times, you become so GOD-CONSCIOUS, you cease to be SELF-CONSCIOUS. The abandonment of fasting has resulted in great spiritual loss to modern Christians.

"How about the Christian's attitude toward wealth?"

matt. 6

19. Do not pile up treasures for yourselves on earth, where they can be lost or stolen from you. 20. But pile up treasures for yourselves in heaven where their value remains forever and there's no way to lose them and no one to steal them. 21. For where your treasure is, there will your heart be also.

TREASURES. Does Jesus sound as though He were denouncing wealth? He isn't. The Bible doesn't forbid wealth. Abraham was possibly the richest man of his day. Certainly Job was fabulously rich after God restored his fortunes. It is not having money or saving for a "rainy day," that Jesus is denouncing, but the SELFISH ACCUMULATION of money and goods for the purpose of living in luxury. God does not want His people chasing the BEST OF THIS WORLD, nor does He want them "feeling at home" on earth. They are to be "pilgrims and strangers," content with a roof over their heads, a bed to sleep in and food in their stomachs. They are not to squander their short time on earth seeking wealth, but rather to invest themselves in Christ. If they allow the "deceitfulness of riches" to blind them, material things will get AHOLD OF THEIR HEARTS (Mk. 4:19). Once that happens, they will never be satisfied, but always want MORE. It's a satanic trap, one that robs the believer of contentment and his single opportunity to qualify for a good job with Jesus. It can knock a man out of the school of kings.

HEAVEN. To help His listeners realize the futility of piling up possessions and money on earth, Jesus says nothing accumulated on earth is safe. In those days, moths got into clothes, rats devoured the grain and worms digested anything placed underground. Gold wasn't safe either. It had to be stored in mud-brick houses, where anyone with a sharp tool could break through and steal it. Today of course, He would speak of inflation, depressions, and governments spending more than they take in. The smart money, says Jesus, is laid up in heaven where the value never diminishes and is guaranteed by God to be safe forever. Simple wisdom dictates that anyone who wants to be truly rich, should invest time, talent and energy to build a fortune in Christ. And there's no limit. A believer can devote his entire life to building such a fortune, becoming filthy rich. The more he accumulates in heaven, the more it pleases God. This is what Paul means when he says, "Set your ambition on things above . . . " (Col 3:2). A man can be as greedy as he wants — BY FAITH.

THE TALE OF TWO TREASURES

Earthly Treasure   **Heavenly Treasure**

A man has but one life to invest, one brief period on earth to make his fortune. But WHERE will he make it? That's Jesus' challenge. Earthly treasure is a foolish investment, says the Lord: 1.) it isn't all that secure, 2.) it really doesn't satisfy the soul, 3.) no matter how much one accumulates, he can't take it with him when he dies. Once that happens, what will he have in heaven? Nothing. He'll arrive there FLAT BROKE. If it is poverty a man fears, why not be poor here for a few years, so as to be rich in heaven for eternity. To be **rich on earth temporarily** and **poverty struck forever** is just about the most foolish decision a man can make.

COMMENT: When Jesus speaks of treasure in heaven, He doesn't tell us exactly what He means by that, at least not in this passage. But it is clear from other references what He has in mind. The Lord died for people. He is "obsessed" with people. This makes people the most valued item in heaven, the real treasure. Luke quotes the Lord as saying, "Use your earthly wealth to make friends for eternity" (Luke 16:9). Christians are thus exhorted to invest their money in advancing the gospel and preparing believers to meet the Lord. In this way they are investing where the Lord invests — in people. The only way earthly treasure can be converted to heavenly treasure is by investing in those who are going to spend eternity with you.

"This seems so obvious you'd think every Christian could see it?"

22. The eye is the floodlight of the body. If your eyes are clear, your whole body is full of light. 23. But if your eyes are blinded, your whole body is full of darkness. And when a man is dark inside, that's the worst kind of darkness, for then he cannot see to make the right decisions.

EYE. You'd think Christians would be eager to store wealth in the BANK OF HEAVEN. But alas, rarely do you find believers thinking or talking about heavenly wealth, much less striving for it. They seem content to focus their lives on careers, families and getting ahead in this world. Why is this? THEY DON'T SEE the folly of earthly treasure. Why not? Their eyes are blinded by material things. They don't have any heavenly vision (Acts 26:19). Unable to SEE THE FACTS as they really are, these Christians are blind to the truth. They see no reason to invest in Christ. So masses of them work furiously day after day, seeking to make themselves SECURE ON EARTH, giving no thought to their futures in heaven. Some

matt. 6

even hold down two jobs, so as to have MORE of this world's goods. It never occurs to them that it would be far wiser to work TWICE AS HARD to accumulate treasure in heaven.

JESUS' EYE ILLUSTRATION

Using the human body and sunlight, the Lord draws a parallel to spiritual vision. To the man with clear eyes, it's as though his insides were flooded with light. To him there is light everywhere. But there is no way for light to penetrate the blind man. Everything in him and around him seems dark. Thus when Christians are blinded by the "deceitfulness of riches," there is no way they can perceive the folly of earthly treasure and the wisdom of heavenly treasure. So they end up investing their time, talent and money on earthly things, totally oblivious to the poverty awaiting them in heaven. If they could only see, they'd forsake the earthly in a flash, in order to gain the heavenly. Poverty in heaven will be no better than it is here. Heaven is NOT the place to be poor.

"Should people really slave for heavenly treasure, just like some do for earthly treasure?"

24. It's obvious a man cannot be the slave of two masters. Therefore one must choose between God and money. For either he will hate God and love money, or he will be devoted to God and despise money. But he can't have it both ways.

> **SLAVE.** The apostle Paul called himself the "bondslave of Jesus Christ" (Phil. 1:1). And this is the way Jesus pictures His disciples — slaves: slaves of money or of God. That's not far-fetched, for we've all seen people SLAVE FOR MONEY. This is why it is so vital to SEE what we're doing with our lives, how we invest them. Christians are free to choose which master they want — but there the freedom ends. Once they decide, they become the SLAVES of the one they've chosen. Now some will protest, saying it's possible to serve two masters, i. e., you can serve God on Sunday and money the other six days. But Jesus says, "THAT'S IMPOSSIBLE." There's no way to SHARE GOD with anyone else. Because the moment you do, YOU BECOME AN IDOLATOR. By definition, idolatry is ANYONE OR ANYTHING we allow to come between us and the Lord. So the choice is just what it appears to be — between a wonderful, personal God Who loves us enough to die for us, or a miserable thing called MONEY. The only reason a Christian would choose money as his master, is because he **simply can't see!** He's blind to the truth.

"What is it that has Christians so worried, that they slave for earthly treasure?"

25. In view of what I've just told you, listen carefully when I tell you not to be so worried about staying alive, that you become anxious over food and drink. God has given you life and a body, and they are

matt. 6

far more important than what to eat or what to wear. If He can give you life and a body, He can certainly provide what is needed for your existence.

WORRIED. Why do people go after earthly treasure so vigorously? Because they feel it will make them secure TOMORROW. They think that if they can accumulate an ABUNDANCE, they will be assured of plenty of food and drink and clothing, and thus ward off the problems of tomorrow. But in the process, they fall into a trap. They never know when they have enough, so they always want more — more security for tomorrow. But Jesus tells His disciples THESE ARE THINGS YOU DON'T HAVE TO WORRY ABOUT. This is God's department. More than that, He FORBIDS them to worry. Worry is totally out of character for the child of God. When a Christian displays anxiety, he is expressing a lack of trust in God's provision. When the believer worries, he is saying, "I doubt that God will take care of me."

LIFE/BODY. Jesus reasons with His disciples about this, saying, God gave you your life in the first place and He sustains it. He also gave you your body and He can sustain that too. If He has the power to give life and equip one with a body, He certainly can do the LESSER PART of supplying what is needed. If one can do the greater, he can do the lesser. That's Jesus' argument. But it goes further than that. The Scriptures speak over and over of God's provision. He has to provide. He has PROMISED to provide. Beyond that He's told us to come to Him for our "daily bread." If we don't see God's part in providing for us, we've got a "blinded eye." **And we'll worry.** But if we have a CLEAR EYE, we'll see that God is a MAN OF HIS WORD and we won't worry. We know He'll come through. He may test us in the process of providing. There may be no food in the house and no money to buy any, but the BEATITUDE MAN will still trust God and not worry. He knows God will come through in the "nick of time".

matt. 6

131

The Christian whose eye is on THINGS, is blinded by the "deceitfulness of riches" (Mk. 4:19). All he can see is how MONEY provides food, drink and clothing. His eye is BLINDED to God's provision. Therefore HE WORRIES about the future and how he will provide for himself and his family. The Christian with the CLEAR EYE, doesn't worry about the basic necessities of life. He sees God's promises in the Word and BELIEVES THEM. His eye is on GOD'S PROVISION and he is filled with peace and joy. So the WORRY-FREE life has to do with SEEING.

matt. 6

26. Look at the wild birds! They don't worry about sowing or reaping or storing food. They don't have to, your heavenly Father feeds them. And you're worth far more to Him than they are. 27. So how can worrying about these things add anything to your life? 28. When it comes to clothes, consider the wild lillies of the field. They don't work. They don't spin. 29. Yet I tell you that Solomon in all his splendor was never dressed as beautifully as one of these. 30. Therefore, if God clothes the flora of the field, which is here today and gone tomorrow, with such dazzling beauty, He will most certainly clothe you, you who have such little faith.

"Look at the wild birds! They don't worry about sowing or reaping or storing food. They don't have to; your heavenly Father feeds them. And you're worth far more to Him than they are."

BIRDS/FLOWERS. Look where Jesus turns to demonstrate God's provision — to the SUBHUMAN WORLD — to birds! To flowers! If you've got an eye to see, says Jesus, these birds and flowers can teach you something. The lesson: if God would care for inferior creatures, such as birds and flowers who have NO FATHER, how much more will He take care of those who are His own! If things like birds and flowers are on the receiving end of God's care; things that are so temporary and without large purpose, how much more will He care for HIS OWN SONS, destined to be His ETERNAL COMPANIONS? The Lord feels this truth is so loudly shouted from nature, that those who can't see it have to be "men of little faith."

matt. 6

133

31. So don't go around worrying and saying, "What are we going to eat?" "What are we going to drink?" "What are we going to wear?" 32. That's what the heathen do. They run after all those things. But you don't have to be like them, for your heavenly Father knows very well what you need.

HEATHEN. Turn on television anytime, day or night, and you'll see an awesome array of advertising geared to the comfort and care of the body. You can't miss the PRE-OCCUPATION. The world is obsessed with the body and how to make it more comfortable, more beautiful. There's alcohol to pep it up, pools to cool it down. Everything needed to feed it, warm it, entertain it and refresh it — yes even make it smell good. And when this load becomes too heavy, there are aspirin and tranquilizers to ease the ache. But all this, says Jesus, IS UNNECESSARY, because our heavenly Father knows all about our needs. So while the heathen are FULL OF ANXIETY, Jesus' disciples should be RELAXED, convinced of God's care for them. So when they run out of money or food in the house, they must not gripe and complain as do the heathen. They know God is merely testing them

matt. 6

and will come through when He's ready. The lifestyle of the believer must be totally different — one that displays complete trust in the Lord. After all, he has a FATHER Who cares for him and the heathen do not.

"What should the Christian do then, with all that energy normally devoted to worrying?"

33. Shift your mind away from those things and set them on God's kingdom, as to how you might help spread it, and on His righteousness, as to how you might live it. Give Him first place in your life and He'll gladly see to it that you get all these things.

SHIFT. Now we come to the heart of the matter. Because God is solidly committed to caring for us, we're FREE from worry over necessities. This doesn't mean we shouldn't PLAN for the future, it is the WORRYING ABOUT IT that Jesus forbids. We are therefore FREE from that worry, free to move our focus from food and clothing to something else. What else? To God and His needs. His mind is on us and our needs, our minds should be on Him and His needs. God's business is to take care of our needs, ours is to take care of His. Instead of stewing and fretting, as some Christians do, we should use that time to fellowship with the Lord, praising Him and presenting others for His blessing. Our minds should occupy with God's plan (kingdom) and trying to live a life that pleases Him (righteousness). With our minds released from worry, we can use that same energy to minister to the Lord. He loves to have us come to Him, thanking Him and acknowledging His goodness, even when there's no food in the house. That kind of faith turns on His shower of blessing — full force.

34. So don't worry about tomorrow. Just live one day at a time and deal with one day's troubles. God will take care of tomorrow as surely as He is taking care of today.

TOMORROW. Jesus may have been smiling when He said this. It's as though He were saying, "Look: if you must worry, limit your worrying to today." Some Christians you see, are going to worry no matter what Jesus teaches and He anticipates this. For those people He has special advice: "If you're going to worry, don't let your worrying include what might happen tomorrow." Naturally, He'd prefer they not worry at all, but if they feel they must, then there are enough TARGETS for worry in the course of a single day. One day can give a dedicated worrier plenty to think about. If he worries about the next day, and nothing happens — he's wasted all that energy. And if it does happen, he's WORRIED TWICE. The smart Christian is the one who PLANS and works toward tomorrow, but doesn't have the least concern about food and shelter. He may not get all the LUXURIES he'd like, but he'll always have food and a roof over his head. Why? Because he's dedicated himself to giving the Lord FIRST PLACE in his life and God has dedicated Himself to providing what is needed to sustain life and body on the earth.

matt. 6

The smart Christian is the one who PLANS and works toward tomorrow, but doesn't have the least concern about food and shelter. He may not get all the LUXURIES he'd like, but he'll always have food and a roof over his head.

matt. 7

"How about our relationships with other Christians? Will the Lord deal with that in this sermon?"

7 1. Do not pass judgment on others or judgment will be passed on you. 2. For just as you judge others, so will you be judged. That is, the severity with which you come down on others, with that same severity will God come down on you.

PASS JUDGMENT. We have come to another famous statement of the Lord, yet one that is badly misunderstood. On first hearing, it sounds as though the Lord is saying, "When it comes to observing what is right or wrong about another person, throw away your common sense and be BLIND to his faults." But that can't possibly be what he means, for in the next breath (vs.6) He tells His disciples to recognize the "dogs" and "pigs" and not to share gospel treasures with them. To do that requires discernment, so as to discriminate between people. Later He will mention

"Do not pass judgment on others or judgment will be passed on you. For just as you judge others, so will you be judged. That is, the severity with which you come down on others, with that same severity will God come down on you."

the "false prophets" and tell them to watch out for them, something they couldn't possible do without making serious judgments about them. If that is so, what then does He mean by not passing judgment? Ah, He doesn't want us climbing up in the JUDGE'S CHAIR, and bringing down the gavel in harsh, condemning judgments about others. It is our ATTITUDE He has in mind. He is forbidding the **harsh censoring** of another because we observe in him a fault, something we feel is really wrong. And we then pounce on that person, pronouncing sentence — at least in our minds.

DON'T PUT YOURSELF IN THE JUDGE'S SEAT

If you presume to put yourself in the judge's seat, says the Lord, don't be surprised to find yourself in the dock. To appoint yourself as THE JUDGE of another, you make yourself SUPERIOR to him, assuming you're qualified to prounce sentence on him. While it is possible for us to observe another's sins, it's ridiculous for us to condemn or censor him, inasmuch as we do not know what's inside him. Only the Holy Spirit knows a person's motives. To climb up in the judge's bench, and JUDGE another's sins, is to play God. If you do, says Jesus, God is going to put you in the dock and judge you the **same way** you judge others.

matt. 7

SAME SEVERITY. Every Christian receives from the Holy Spirit the ABILITY TO DISCERN ERROR. It is a gift from God, enabling us to recognize what is true and false, what is good or evil in another person. Without this ability we would fall prey to false teachers, as well as being unable to counsel or correct other believers. But the Spirit DOES NOT give us this ability so that we can be critical of others, or to judge them — but so we can be GENEROUS TOWARD THEM. God is generous with us. He beholds ALL OF OUR SINS and yet doesn't pounce on us. He works with us TO HELP US OVERCOME. It's amazing how GENTLE He is with us, especially when there's so much awful stuff in us for Him to behold. He wants us to be like Himself — loving people **in spite of their sins.** For every wrong we see in another, God sees the SAME in us **and hundreds more.** Therefore, if we are generous about the sins of others, we can expect God to be generous about our sins. But if we HARSHLY JUDGE others for their sins, we can expect God to be HARSH with us concerning our sins until we start displaying a more gracious attitude. Bear in mind we are discussing SINS, not sin. SIN (guilt) was cared for at Calvary. SINS have to do with fellowship, fellowship with God and our brethren.

"Our judging does seem ridiculous when viewed in the light of our own sins."

3. Why focus on that speck of sawdust in your brother's eye and pay no attention to the log in your own eye? 4. How can you presume to say to your brother, "Let me get that speck out of your eye," when all the time you're blinded by that log in your own eye? 5. You hypocrite! First, get that log out of your own eye, then you'll be able to see clearly enough to remove the speck from your brother's eye.

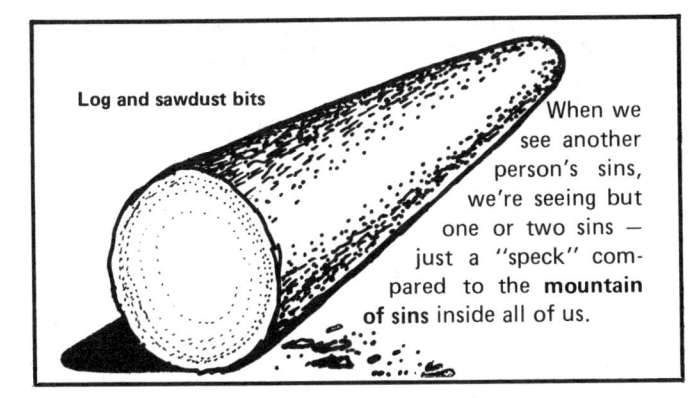

matt. 7

Log and sawdust bits. When we see another person's sins, we're seeing but one or two sins — just a "speck" compared to the **mountain of sins** inside all of us.

SPECK/LOG. Visit a sawmill. Watch a huge log press into the whirling saw. Dust flies in all directions. Pick up a piece. Look at it. Then look at the log. What a difference! That difference is the basis of Jesus' teaching. When we see another's sins, we're seeing but one or two sins — just a "speck" compared to the MOUNTAIN OF SINS inside all of us. So the Lord says, before you judge your brother, TAKE A LOOK AT THE MOUNTAIN inside you, a mountain that is the product of your old nature. One good look at that awful mess, which God sees, and we're not so prone to pounce. His little "speck" doesn't look so bad when compared to our "LOG." Seeing your own AWFUL MESS first, should put you in mind to HELP HIM, not judge him. When the apostle Paul says, "Esteem others better than yourselves," this is what he has in mind (Phil. 2:3). By comparing a brother's one or two visible sins against the mountain of evil in one's own heart, almost forces him to regard others better than himself. One day we may be able to look into other people's hearts. But until that day, we must not judge.

HYPOCRITE. As students in the SCHOOL OF KINGS, it's part of our training to learn how to DISCERN AND DISCRIMINATE. In fact, we should always be working on our powers of discernment,

matt. 7

sharpening them. We need to be able to make CRITICAL EVALUATIONS OF OTHERS — but not to judge them. It's for our protection when we encounter evil. We have to distinguish between what is true and what is false. Instead of judging a brother, we are to help him overcome his fault (Gal. 6:1); but not until we have first taken a good look at what our evil natures have wrought in us. Only then can we set about to restore a brother. But if we use our DISCERNING POWERS to focus on a brother's faults and pass judgment, WE'RE HYPOCRITES, says the Lord. We're no better than the PHARISEES who were phony in their giving, praying and fasting. We're phonies too, when we assume the ROLE OF JUDGES, and then use our DISCERNING POWERS to put down a brother, who in reality is no worse than we are. The Lord hates such hypocrisy. It's like the "pot calling the kettle black." We have to ask ourselves, "How would I fare if God judged me with the same harshness with which I judge others!" Wow!

"What about those who care nothing for the Lord? Surely we're to judge between them and those who love Him, aren't we?"

6. Don't give any of our sacred things to the dogs. Don't throw our pearls to the pigs. If you do, they will simply trample on them and turn around and tear you to pieces.

PEARLS. When Jesus ordered the 70 to go ahead of Him into the various cities of Israel, He instructed them to judge between two kinds of people — those worthy to hear their message and those who were not (Luke 10;1-11). Similarly, the Lord is here instructing His disciples to watch out for the DOGS and PIGS. These are people, of course. It might seem strange to hear Him use such words right after telling us not to **pass judgment** on others. But again, He is NOT telling them to pass judgment, but to BE DIS-

CERNING. The context is DISCERNMENT. There are PIGS out there, He says, and DOGS. You must watch out for them. If you can't tell the difference, you're likely to share some SACRED THINGS with people who have no business hearing them. There are TREASURES in the Word of God, riches of revelation that belong ONLY to the saints. God does not want them offered to outsiders, people who have no capacity to appreciate them. Instead, they are likely to despise them and even make fun of the Christians offering them.

matt. 7

PIGS/DOGS. Harsh words, these. The Lord is thinking of WILD PIGS, viscious animals so fierce, they can rout panthers and cheetahs. With their long, razor-sharp teeth, they could easily slash a man to pieces. The DOGS He refers to are not cuddly lap-dogs, but wild mongrels that travel in vicious packs and scavenge the dumps. They're dangerous, too. With such figures, Jesus pictures those who hear the gospel, but defiantly reject it. They are people with no genuine interest in the Lord, but actually regard Him with contempt. These dogs laugh at the truths of God, making fun of those who love Jesus. But that's to be expected in a PIG WORLD. The masses of mankind have no interest in the things of God, but only in the SLOP of the world. As God views things, most of mankind prefers to wallow in the mud of materialism, despising the gems of the gospel. So, in effect Jesus is saying, "I don't want you sharing the riches of revelation, the pearls of the faith-life, with these DOGS. Like the pigs of the forest, they have no way to appreciate what they're hearing. They'll just spit them out and lash out at you!"

matt. 7

142

PIGS AND PROSPECTS

See the two kinds of people: **Pigs & Prospects**. Those with a genuine heart for God are real prospects. They're entitled to the **pearls,** But those with NO HEART for God, are not. They are entitled to the GOSPEL INVITATION, the invitation to be saved — **and that's all**. The gospel invitation is NOT A PEARL. It's not a gem. By way of radio, television and the printing press, the earth is covered (like dust) with the invitation to Christ. It's everywhere, almost as common as dirt itself. And this is how God wants it. We're to share the INVITATION WITH EVERYONE, but not the riches of revelation. They are to be guarded and enjoyed only by the family of God. They are the FAMILY JEWELS.

DON'T GIVE. Doesn't Jesus want the gospel shared with everyone? Indeed — but only the GOOD NEWS. What's that? That God loves them, wants them and has provided a way for them to come to Him — CHRIST! They are to get the INVITATION ONLY — nothing more. If we go beyond that, we run the risk of casting our pearls before wild pigs. Therefore, just as a good car salesman QUALIFIES HIS PROSPECTS, so are we to DISCERN (recognize) the kind of people with whom we are sharing the gospel. Jesus is the MAGNET

OF HEAVEN. We're to HOLD UP CHRIST and LET HIM "draw all men unto Me" (John 12:32). If people really want heaven, they'll "taste and see that the Lord is good" (Psa. 34:8). If they like the taste and want more, then they're entitled to the pearls. But if they don't want Jesus — THEY'RE PIGS! Christians MUST LEARN to distinguish between PIGS and REAL PROSPECTS and withhold the riches of Christianity from those who do not qualify. For those in the SCHOOL OF KINGS, learning to distinguish between pigs and prospects, is an ELEMENTARY LEVEL of discernment. Later the Lord will speak of RECOGNIZING FALSE TEACHERS. That is a higher level and a lot harder.

"Hey! This is some kind of a life! Where do we get the power to live this kind of a life?"

7. Be persistent in asking and you'll receive what you're praying for. Be persistent in seeking and you'll find what you're looking for. Keep on knocking and the door will open to you. 8. For everyone who asks persistently, receives; and he who seeks persistently, finds; and to everyone who keeps knocking, the door opens.

ASKING. To understand Jesus' words, the context of the Sermon on the Mount must be before us — becoming like our Father in heaven. If we're honest with ourselves, we'll admit we're a long way from being what we'd like to be. This means we must make a lot of changes. But changes don't come easily. We can't change ourselves any more than a brain surgeon can operate on his own brain. The world can't help, it has no righteousness at all. Therefore, God alone can help us be what we ought to be — like Christ. The Lord is teaching us: if we are to receive what we need for changing into our Father's likeness, we must ASK . . . SEEK . . . KNOCK and be persistent about it. Those 3 verbs are PRESENT IMPERATIVE in the Greek, which means we've got to keep on asking, seeking and knocking. But why would God make us come to Him again and again? Doesn't He want to give us the things we need to become like Him? Of course — BUT WE'RE NOT READY TO RECEIVE THEM. Our continual coming to Him is part of the process of getting us ready.

COMMENT: Prayer is not the chief business of American Christians. Their chief business is being BUSY: busy with families, homes, jobs, careers, financial security and getting ahead in this life. We live in a non-praying environment, surrounded by a hustle/bustle society that is too busy to pray. Modern life in this land literally excludes prayer. As a result, believers are FORCED TO TAKE TIME to be holy. They have to TAKE TIME to go to God for what they need. And they cannot do this occasionally, says Jesus, and expect anything from God. They must be persistent about it. By persistence He means, MAKE IT YOUR BUSINESS.

RECEIVES. On the surface it sounds like persistent prayer brings the believer everything he asks for. Far from it, there are strings attached to Jesus' promises, conditions to be met. Yet some seize upon His words, "Whatever you ask in My name, I will do it," as giving them a blank check (John 14:14). So they carefully tack on the end of their prayer list, "In Jesus' name!" This, they feel, obligates God to give them what they ask for. That is sheer nonsense. God is not a MAGIC LAMP that one rubs with the words, "In Jesus' name." He wants those who ACHE TO BE LIKE JESUS, to come to Him asking for what is needed to change them. He is thrilled to answer them. The Lord is not discussing daily bread and our wants here. He has already done that (6:11). The ASKING... SEEKING... KNOCKING in this passage, is for help to be holy; to overcome evil; to become Beatitude men and women. When that is our ambition, we can seek and ask and knock (a single package actually) and know God's answer is ready.

matt. 7

"Is God reluctant to answer? Do we have to beg Him for what we want? Is that why persistence is needed?"

9. What man among you, should his son ask for bread, will give him a stone? 10. Or if he asks for a fish, will give him a deadly snake? 11. If you then, evil as you are, know how to give your children what is best for them, how much more will your Father in heaven give what is good to those who ask Him?

BREAD/FISH. To make sure His disciples don't miss the point, the Lord resorts to a ridiculous contrast. He presents a familiar picture to their minds — that of a hungry child coming to his father for bread. In those days bread was made of whole grains and often baked in small round loaves (individual portions). They looked like rocks. So Jesus asks, would ANY HUMAN FATHER give his hungry boy a rock to eat? And if he asked for a fish, give him a deadly snake? One is impossible to eat, the other poisonous. Of course not. That's the point. If men, who are only evil (selfish by nature), would give **only good things** to their children, HOW MUCH MORE would God give only good things to His? It would violate God's nature to give anything that would hurt or harm. So here's the key: God, BEING GOOD, can only give good gifts. BEING WISE, he can only give what is BEST FOR US. So if we ask for that which is not good for us, we won't get it no matter how much we ask, seek or knock. And when we ask for the BEST THINGS, we don't get them until we're READY to receive them. The BEST GIFTS are those which help us become **like Christ**.

matt. 7

TWO KINDS OF HEAVENLY GIFTS

Universal Gifts
(no prayer needed)

Children
Crops
Houses, Cars, Clothes
Jobs, Careers
Financial Security
Recreational Joys
Success
Rain and Sun

Family Gifts
(only by prayer)

Salvation (Holy Spirit)
Forgiveness
Deliverance from Evil
Strength to Overcome
Power to Resist Satan
Discernment
Understanding of Word
Wisdom

Observe two kinds of gifts flowing from heaven — UNIVERSAL GIFTS and FAMILY GIFTS. One set is received without any prayer at all, the other is obtained through prayer only. UNIVERSAL GIFTS are secured by working. A man can raise crops, a mother can have babies, and people can enjoy pleasures and possessions simply by working for them. Even the sun and rain come without prayer. But FAMILY GIFTS are another matter. Salvation (The Holy Spirit) must be sought from God (Luke 11:13) The same is true of deliverance from evil. The strength to overcome weaknesses, as well as wisdom and discernment, must come from God. FAMILY GIFTS ARE FOR BELIEVERS ONLY, intended to help them mature in Christ. They must be sought persistently. Don't be puzzled by prayerless Christians who prosper in this life. They are simply enjoying the UNIVERSAL GIFTS. Devoid of family gifts, their lives do not change. Do not envy them, for CHANGE is the name of the game in the SCHOOL OF KINGS.

DOOR OPENS. Feebleness in prayer produces powerless Christians. Wanting to reverse that, God makes PERSISTENCE a condition for His answers. Only those persistent in seeking HIS BEST, get the help they need. Through persistence, believers get to know the Lord so well, they understand how HE FEELS AND THINKS. As a result, they soon learn how to ask for those things God is **eager to give.** Once they reach that high ground, it then becomes true, "Whatever you ask in My name, I will do it!" **But not until then.** We ought to be thankful God doesn't give us everything we ask for. Some of our lives would really be messed up if He did. For it would be like giving matches and razor blades to toddlers. One writer says, "If God were pledged to give me everything I asked for, I would never pray again." That man didn't want such awesome responsibility. Think what you might ask for when angry with someone! Praise God He knows what's best for us and answers according to His wisdom, not ours.

matt. 7

147

"Once we know how to ask God for the BEST THINGS, those that help us mature in Christ, what effect should this have on our life-styles?"

12. Therefore, in view of your astonishing resources through prayer, start treating others as you would like them to treat you — and do it in every situation. When you live by this principle, you fulfill the Law and the Prophets, when it comes to loving your neighbor.

THEREFORE. There is a connection between persistent praying and the awesome principle the Lord has just set forth. It takes supernatural power to treat others as you would like to be treated. But that is available to us. If we accept this principle, this rule (the golden rule) and determine to live by it — we become so totally different, **that we appear as different people.** That's what God seeks to do with us,

matt. 7

148

REMAKE US so that we become like SOMEONE ELSE — Jesus. It doesn't happen overnight, of course, for people grow more slowly than trees. But if we really work at living by this rule, more and more of Jesus' character will be seen in us. If you want to make a quick check of your progress in the SCHOOL OF KINGS, observe from time to time, just how much your attitude toward others has changed. The more we become like Jesus, the more we treat people as we would like to be treated. It takes supernatural power to live by this rule, but that's exactly what's available to us when we ask God for His BEST for us.

> The more we become like Jesus, the more we treat people as we would like to be treated. It takes supernatural power to live by this rule, but that's exactly what's available to us when we ask God for His BEST for us.

matt. 7

TREAT OTHERS. In Old Testament times there was a similar rule, but it was in the NEGATIVE FORM, "Don't do to others what you wouldn't wish them to do to you." That is, if you don't want others to be critical of you, don't be critical yourself. Or, if you don't like to be abused, or cheated or gossipped about, don't do those things to others. Inasmuch as Old Testament believers were equipped with OLD NATURES ONLY, God's rules were RESTRAINTS. They were given THOU SHALT NOTS. However, with New Testament Christians equipped with the "divine nature," the Lord no longer teaches THOU SHALT NOT, but THOU SHALT DO. The DO CONCEPT is easy to understand. All you have to do is put yourself in the other fellow's shoes and ask: "How would I like to be treated in this situation?" Then do it. That way, your instinct to look out for NUMBER ONE, can guide you in how to behave toward others. Following this principle, if you enjoy being loved by others, then love others yourself. If you like being treated honestly, fairly and with respect, then treat others that way. Live by this principle, says Jesus, and you won't need any other rules.

LAW/PROPHETS. This principle is so wide, says the Lord, it fulfills the law and the prophets. This is what the law and the prophets are all about; what they were trying to accomplish in the lives of the people. As Bishop Ryle once wrote: "If we follow this principle, it settles a hundred different points. It eliminates the necessity of laying down endless rules for our conduct in specific situations." The Lord insisted that He had not come to "destroy the law and the prophets, but to fulfill them" (Matt. 5:17). The GOLDEN RULE fulfills both — at least with regard to loving one's neighbor. Someone asks, "If we live like this, won't people take advantage?" Sure. But with **God's promise** to supply our needs through prayer, we don't have to worry about being exploited. **We're backed**

matt. 7

by an unlimited supply. We don't have to have the best — or be the first — or have the most. We're glad to see the other person get it . . . for he's being treated as we would like to be treated. If someone beats us at the traffic signal or gets ahead of us at work, we don't care because we desire for others what we would like for ourselves. Wow! What a transformation takes place when we live by this principle! We become totally different people!

HOW THIS PRINCIPLE MAKES US GLOW

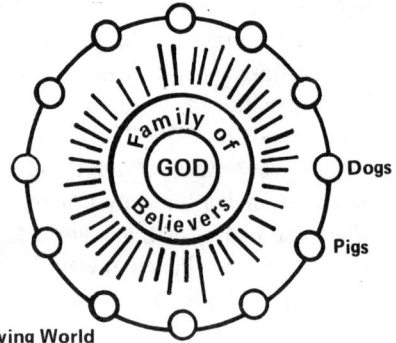

Family of Believers — GOD — Dogs — Pigs

The Unbelieving World

The Christian's spirit is embossed with two unshakeables: 1.) that God is his Father, 2.) that all other Christians are his brothers and sisters. With God at the center, believers form a FAMILY around the Lord. Then there's a wider circle — the outsiders. Sprinkled here and there among them, are the DOGS AND PIGS. The Lord has already told us what to do about them. When we live by the golden principle just laid out by Jesus, we GLOW like a huge light bulb. At the center is God the filament. Around Him, we form the GLASS SHELL that makes the LIGHT BULB. Our glowing lives radiate Christ, for we have gradually changed into His likeness (Eph. 5:8). Living by this principle, we provide the world (the outer circle) with the only spiritual light available. Apart from glowing Christians, there is no way for the world to see God.

"Wow! What a sermon! How will Jesus challenge His listeners to get going on this kind of a life?"

matt. 7

13. If you wish to go to heaven, you must enter through a very narrow gate. For you see, the road to destruction has a big wide gate and is a multilane freeway that easily handles the many who go that way. 14. It is because the road to life has such a small gate and narrow road, that only a few ever find it.

MUST ENTER. The Lord confronts His listeners with decision time, putting the choice before them in striking terms. He uses a metaphor familiar to everyone — that of a wide road with its big gate and a narrow road with its tiny gate. We're to visualize the masses of humanity as traveling along the HIGHWAY OF HUMAN LIFE, a highway everyone enters by way of physical birth. Along the highway, signs are posted that speak of the kingdom of heaven. Those traveling the freeway glance at these signs from time to time, paying little attention to them. Then the freeway bends. A final sign says, HEAVEN: NEXT TURN OFF. As one gets closer, the turnoff is onto a small narrow road with a tiny gate. It doesn't look too inviting. Besides, it's been said there's persecution on that road and you have to live by the golden rule. With talk of denying yourself and turning the other cheek, it seems more reasonable to stay on the freeway and continue with the crowds, even though other signs warn, DESTRUCTION AHEAD. By way of this imagery, the Lord is saying, "If you want to go to heaven, you've got to TURN OFF the freeway, go through the small gate and get on the narrow road that leads to life (the kingdom)."

FREEWAY. Yes, the freeway looks like the easier way to go. But that's because it's so spacious, spacious in tolerance and permissiveness. It's wide enough to let every man have his own ideas as to what's right and wrong. There's plenty of room for

matt. 7

all kinds of morals and the other guy's religion. As long as the freeway traveler feels he's as "good as the next guy," he's sure he'll get by OK. It's so nice not to have to deal with your sins or self-righteousness. All a person has to do is follow the inclinations of his heart, regardless of what the Bible might say. As a result, this road is packed bumper to bumper with the masses of humanity following each other like sheep. Born onto this freeway, the average man knows nothing except going to school, getting a job, getting married, raising a family, preparing for retirement, a meaningless sequence with a grave at the end. Everyone does it, even the otherwise brilliant doctors, lawyers and scientists. None asks, "Where is this road taking me? What am I doing here?" Instead, they shun Jesus' invitation and blindly follow the herd into hell. To them, it makes no sense to leave the big, wide freeway to get on that tiny narrow road.

THE TWO ROADS

Heaven

Human Stream Highway

Hell

Here are the two roads. The freeway of human life, packed with the world's billions, is headed for destruction (HELL). At some point the travelers learn of Jesus' invitation to go to heaven. But to go there, they MUST LEAVE THE PACK, get off the freeway and boldly turn onto a little side road that looks almost deserted. The road to heaven isn't very big, says Jesus, because SO FEW are interested in My way of life. The SCHOOL OF KINGS sounds like torture compared to the easy road they're currently traveling. So they IGNORE the warning signs: DESTRUCTION AHEAD. They reassure themselves, saying, "There's no way a good God would allow the bulk of humanity to go to hell!"

matt. 7

NARROW ROAD. Look at the people on the narrow road. They're few and they're strange. They hate their sins, their greeds and selfish ambition. They don't strike back when abused. They don't want anything from the world, it's just a school to them. Knowing the road they're traveling is paved with sacrifice, they gladly forsake the pleasures of the world, preferring the reproach of Christ. They're willing even to put aside their families, if that's what it takes to follow Christ. Not willing to follow the FREEWAY CROWDS down the road of destruction, they DARE TO GET OFF the freeway and go through the tiny gate. They want to be among the VERY FEW of the world's billions (no one knows how many that is) that end up in heaven. They hate to see the MANY go to hell, but it's clear they do so by their own free choice. It's sad to learn the bulk of mankind prefers the broad road to destruction rather than the narrow road to heaven.

COMMENT: Most movies and novels have happy endings, with their heroes riding off into the sunset. But Jesus' Sermon doesn't end with any lofty ideas of how good man is or how he's finally going to make it. Instead, it ends with the failure of man to know the God who made him. Even when an escape from the world's fate is opened to him, he won't take it. This is why Jesus told His disciples that the WORLD (bulk of mankind) would hate them. He knew the masses of the world would remain the enemies of God, with no desire to be anything else. This message is not popular today. Some just can't believe a good God would do this. But God has no choice. There's no way He can spend eternity with those who don't want Him. Yet man has a choice. Anytime he wishes, he can get off the SUICIDE ROAD. Jesus is saying, "DO IT NOW!"

"Once we get off the freeway and onto the narrow road, will we become the targets of false teachers?"

15. Watch out for false prophets who come to you

matt. 7

wearing sheep's clothing. In reality, they are savage wolves just waiting to devour you. 16. You can recognize them by what they produce, just as you can identify a tree by what it produces. Now who is going to try to pick grapes off a thorn bush or gather figs from thistles? The difference is unmistakable. 17. But when it comes to good and bad trees, they look so much alike, you have to check their fruit to identify them. 18. A healthy tree cannot produce bad fruit and a sick tree cannot produce good fruit. 19. Once the fruit is checked, the trees producing bad fruit are cut down and burned. 20. Similarly, when looking at teachers, the way to distinguish between the true and false is by checking the fruit each produces.

But when it comes to good and bad trees, they look so much alike, you have to check their fruit to identify them. A healthy tree cannot produce bad fruit and a sick tree cannot produce good fruit.

matt. 7

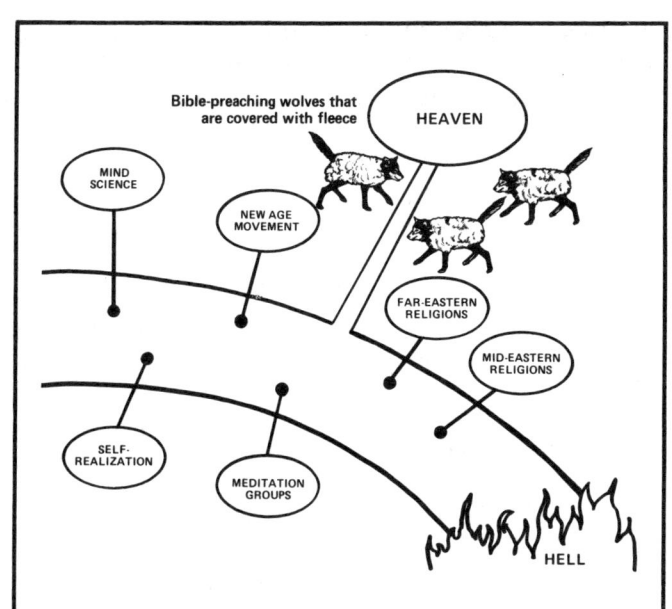

155

It shocked us to learn the bulk of mankind prefers to stay on the freeway. But once we're off the freeway, we come under a peculiar kind of attack. Teachers, who look like true Christians, will call to us, asking us to turn aside from the narrow road and follow their brand of "Christianity." Some will claim theirs is the only true church, others will claim Jesus is not God, but a SON OF GOD, like the rest of us. Still more will teach that you have to **add something** to your faith to be saved... whether baptisms, Sabbath-keeping or speaking in tongues. Concerning these teachers, the apostle Paul says, "Let them be accursed" (Gal. 1:9). Observe these teachers are NOT on the road, but stand off on one side. They are not God's sheep, but actually wolves dressed up to look like sheep. Down on the FREEWAY, there are plenty of religious merchants (cults), but they don't pretend to be anything but what they say they are: MEDITATION groups, MINDSCIENCE, NEW AGE MOVEMENT, SELF-REALIZATION, etc. They don't use the Bible to deceive as do the WOLVES who are after the sheep. Watch out, says Jesus, they're dangerous!

matt. 7

WATCH OUT. Those false teachers, says the Lord, are wolves disguised as sheep — and they can appear in your very midst. In Jesus' day, wolves were the deadly enemies of sheep. A shepherd had to keep his eyes open, because sheep are so defenseless. A wolf can scatter a flock and kill a number of them before the shepherd realizes he's there. With these words, Jesus is saying a flock of Christians can be at the mercy of either a good shepherd or a paid wolf. A good shepherd (pastor) will feed his people from the Word, whereas a false teacher is likely to divide (even destroy) sheep with his error. With the advent of TELEVISION, there are now big flocks participating in the electronic church. Very tempting to modern wolves. The clever teacher is keenly aware that God's people are GULLIBLE, due to their scant knowledge of the Bible. They'll believe almost anything, if the teacher is pious, uses the right cliches and says, "Praise the Lord" frequently. Some have gone so far as to say, "God told me that you were to give X amount of dollars to my ministry." A shrewd teacher can easily get God's people to believe "grapes grow on thorn bushes," and separate them from their money.

DISGUISED. A wolf is dangerous enough, but disguise him as a sheep and the flock is in real trouble. This is why believers MUST LEARN to discern between good and evil in another, even though they do not pass judgment. If they can't discern evil, they are "sitting ducks." Of course, if someone comes saying, "Forget about Jesus. There are lots of Christs — and I'm one of them," the sheep would laugh and say, "Yeah, and figs grow on thistles, too!" They wouldn't be fooled. But let the man come DISGUISED, wearing a FLEECE of credentials, a big testimony, a BIG NAME, all the right phrases as well as persuasive charm, and the sheep will fall in line behind him. Jesus is warning us: **"DON'T BE FOOLED BY APPEARANCES!"** No matter how charming or godly a man

APPEARS TO BE, or how many degrees he has, look under the fleece to see what really lives there. One sure test, says the Lord, is watching to see WHAT FRUIT a man's ministry produces. If he actually produces BEATITUDE MEN AND WOMEN, he's a good teacher. But if there are no changed lives, be careful. You could have a wolf in your midst.

matt. 7

A good shepherd (pastor) will feed his people from the Word, whereas a false teacher is likely to divide (even destroy) sheep with his error. No matter how charming or godly a man APPEARS TO BE, or how many degrees he has, look under the fleece to see what really lives there.

matt. 7

IDENTIFY. In Matthew 24, the Lord sounded the same warning, but in a context that applies directly to us today. In fact, He opened His discussion saying, "Take heed that no man deceive you" (Vs. 4). The Lord went on to explain how the gospel would be preached world-wide, but at the same time, there would be a **RISE of false teachers** that would "deceive many"(Vs. 11). For myself, I learned long ago, the best way to protect myself against error, was to KNOW THE BOOK. I don't mean simply reading and acquiring Bible knowledge, but reading the Bible WITH THE LORD, especially the gospels. Why? To get used to His voice. The Lord says, "My sheep hear My voice and they follow Me,...another they will not follow, but flee from him: for they know not the voice of strangers" (John 10:4, 5). Jesus is the true shepherd and it is possible to get so used to His voice, as you read the Word, that when something false comes along, your spirit says, "Oh oh!" SO get into the Word on a daily basis. Become familiar with the voice of the Spirit (1st John 2:27). Then, like a bank teller, you'll be able to spot the phony, because you're so familiar with the real thing. We're all going to need this protection in the days ahead.

"Suppose we develop the ability to recognize false teachers, what's to keep us from fooling ourselves? Will the Lord comment on that before He ends the sermon?"

21. Not all who say to Me, "Lord, Lord," will enter the kingdom of heaven. They may sound like real Christians, but they're not. Only those who do the will of My Father in heaven will be admitted. 22. When that day comes, and I'm speaking of judgment day, many will say to Me, "Lord, Lord, did we not prophesy in Your name, and in Your name cast out demons, and did we not perform many miracles in Your name?" 23. Then I will tell them flat out, **"At no time have I ever known you. Get away from Me you evil doers."**

matt. 7

LORD, LORD. Having come to the end of His sermon, the Lord closes with a final caution to His disciples. Above He warned them of false teachers, but here He cautions them against FOOLING THEMSELVES. To reinforce the awfulness of self-deception, He shocks them. "MANY," He says, will cry out to Him on JUDGMENT DAY thinking they are entitled to enter the kingdom on the basis of what they SAY to Him. And MANY will find themselves EXCLUDED because of something MISSING in their lives. They have NOT DONE GOD'S WILL. Thinking they have been in the center of God's will, they make LOUD CLAIMS, citing all the things they've DONE in Jesus' name. "Lord! Lord!" they cry with great emotion, for these are not cold, unemotional people, but vigorous, enthusiastic workers. Recalling their fruitful ministries, they speak of their supernatural fireworks: prophecy, exorcisms and miracles. Talk about the supernatural — they've done it all. Experiences galore, healings of all kinds. But alas, these supernatural ministries do not impress Jesus. "You do all this in My name," He says. "Strange, but I don't even know your names. Never have." What's shocking is — **there are so many of them!**

MIRACLES. The Lord doesn't deny these people have had great, supernatural ministries. He knows all about their successes. Obviously they've performed amazing deliverances and seen many healings. That's not the problem. The trouble is — they've fooled themselves into thinking RESULTS somehow equal true spirituality. That success in serving the Lord is the same thing as godliness and poverty of spirit. They've deluded themselves by thinking that their POWERFUL MINISTRIES mean they are truly submitted to Jesus' lordship. Enamored with success, they substitute it for obedience. To them, RESULTS are everything. To them performing SPIRITUAL WONDERS means they have a genuine heart-commitment. For that reason,

matt. 7

they insist they belong in the kingdom. But Jesus says, "No. You have correct doctrine, your works are great, but your HEARTS are not with Me." There is no way anyone can enter the kingdom on the basis of a supernatural ministry, no matter how big or successful it may be.

Here's a man with marvelous talents from the Lord. Using those talents, he builds a spectacular ministry bringing forth supernatural RESULTS. The success is so astonishing, he becomes enamored with it. He measures his spirituality by the size of his operation, assuming he's in the center of God's will. He doesn't see how he can miss the kingdom. But he fails to see that his SUCCESS is **due entirely** to God's working and the gifts He's received. The true disciple, on the other hand says, "Lord all this is Your doing, not mine. My job is to be submitted to You. My desire is not for success, but to be LIKE YOU and PLEASE YOU in what I do and say." The true disciple cares little whether his work is BIG OR SMALL. His confidence is not based on the **results of a ministry,** but on his TOTAL SUBMISSION to Jesus. Aware that GOD PRODUCES THE RESULTS, he places **no confidence** in his success. This man's entrance into the kingdom is assured because of his heart-commitment. The other man is excluded because all he's got to offer the Lord are words about his supernatural successes.

matt. 7

GET AWAY FROM ME. The Lord is eager to spend eternity with those who really want Him. He is not simply looking for workers. He wants those who are committed to HIM, not committed to success. **He can make anyone successful.** It's not uncommon to hear of ministers, with fine ministries, who discover years later, **they were never saved.** They've worked FOR the Lord, but they didn't work WITH HIM. They hadn't **obeyed God** in committing their lives to Jesus. Their HEADS believed in Him, but their HEARTS didn't. When judgment day arrives, they will find themselves excluded from the kingdom. They will protest, claiming they should be admitted on the basis of their supernatural successes. But Jesus won't have them anywhere near Him. "Get away from Me," He says, calling them "EVILDOERS." You would think it would be impossible for anyone involved in the WONDERS of Christianity to fool themselves so utterly, but Jesus says "MANY" will do this. Are such workers around us today? Of course. Who are they? I don't know. Only Jesus knows on what a person is basing his confidence for entering the kingdom.

"In other words, these people have built their lives on the wrong foundation? They've based their confidence on results and successes, rather than in the Lord Himself — is that right?"

24. Therefore, those who listen to My words and build their lives on them will be like the wise man who had the good sense to build his house on solid rock. 25. Even though the rains came and the flood waters rose and the winds beat against his house — it didn't give way, because it was anchored to the rock. 26. But those who hear My words and do not build their lives on them, are like the foolish man who built his house on bare sand. 27. Then, when the rains came and the floods rose and the wind blasted his house, it collapsed in total ruin.

matt. 7

THEREFORE. Here's a word we all appreciate — THEREFORE. The Lord is about to drive home the point with an illustration his hearers couldn't fail to understand. His sermon ends with the well known parable of the wise and foolish builders. The wise man dug down and built his house on solid rock. The foolish man built his house on bare sand. Once the two houses were completed, one looked as sturdy as the other. An observer wouldn't notice any difference between them, since the foundations are below ground and unseen. No, there's no way to know the difference UNTIL THE TEST COMES. In this case it's a BIG STORM, with its rain, flood and wind. Only then is it revealed there's no foundation under the house of the fool. In the same way, the Lord is cautioning His listeners to make sure the house they're building (their lives) is on solid rock. And what is that SOLID ROCK? Jesus and His words. Again and again, throughout the gospels, Jesus urges people to lay hold of His words. "If a man love Me, He will keep My words" (John 14:23). We must build our lives on Jesus and His words, the wonderful words of life. Christians often sing this truth "On Christ the solid rock I stand, all other ground is sinking sand!"

FOOLISH MAN. You wouldn't think it possible to know all about Jesus, be doctrinally sound and then build your life on anything other than the Lord. But it happens. The Lord has already told us that even those with supernatural ministries can deceive themselves to the place where they build their lives on results, rather than on Him. In one place, Jesus taught, "My words are spirit and they are life" (John 6:63). Here He is saying in effect, "Make a heart-commitment to Me on the basis of My words and build your lives on them!" In this way, Jesus' words become the FOUNDATION of the believer's life. The man who builds on any other foundation IS A FOOL, for when the storms of life come (or the judgment), it won't stand up to the

TEST. The Lord feels this is so urgent, He makes it the FINAL WORD of His sermon. Anyone reading these lines should take inventory and make sure his life is solidly built on the ROCK, Christ Jesus. This is not an area where anyone can afford to take a chance. So the final caution is — DON'T FOOL YOURSELF!

"Wow! What a sermon!
How did the people react to such words?"

28. When Jesus had finished saying these things, the crowds were astonished at His teaching. 29. He was so utterly different from their Bible teachers, that they were rocked by the extraordinary authority with which He taught.

ASTONISHED. As Jesus' last words echoed across the valley, the people stood in silence, frozen to the spot. They scarcely knew what to say to one another. They had never heard such things. Not a few must have had burning hearts, as did the two men on the road to Emmaus (Luke 24:32). The question nagging at their minds was, "WHO IS THIS MAN?" They thought they knew Him as Jesus, a Jew from Galilee, a man with no formal education. But here He was, sweeping aside all their rabbis had taught them. Israel was a "nation under God" with no separation of church and state. There were thousands of teachers from one end of the land to the other, all rabbis. Israelites were raised to respect Moses and the law, with the rabbis' teachings forming the basis of their lives. But here is THIS MAN, overpowering them with His own teachings, wiping out much of what the rabbis had taught them. Never had they seen such a man before, never had they heard such things before. Yet they don't react against Him, because they are OVERWHELMED by the awesome authority with which He was teaching them.

matt. 7

AUTHORITY. The teachers of Israel had NO AUTHORITY of their own. Their authority came from quoting others; Moses and the prophets and leaders of rabbinical schools. They simply passed on what others said, explaining the traditions just as they themselves had been taught. So now the crowds are DUMBFOUNDED by Jesus' OWN authority. He dared to contradict their teachers. "YOU HAVE HEARD THAT IT WAS SAID . . . BUT I SAY UNTO YOU . . .!" Then He proceeded to set them straight on murder, divorce, adultery and retaliation, etc. As He did so, they sensed everything He was saying was true. The reason? In some mysterious way they felt they were listening to God. Of course, the Lord never once told them He was God — at least not in so many words. Still it was clear that He was SOMEHOW one with God. It blew their minds to think they were listening to a man, a fellow Jew, and at the same time had the feeling He was God. It haunted them. You see, He sounded like God. And some of the things He said definitely implied that He was God.

COMMENT: While Jesus never once told them He was God, some of His statements planted that impression in their minds. For example, when He said **many** would say TO HIM on judgment day, "Did we not prophesy . . cast out demons . . . and perform miracles in Your name?" He told them to get away from Him. "I've never known you," He said. Please observe where this takes place — AT THE DOOR OF HEAVEN! Jesus sees Himself as the JUDGE, deciding who enters heaven and who doesn't. Yet, everyone knew that GOD ALONE is the Judge of mankind. So here we have Jesus, by implication, putting Himself in the place of God. He said similar things throughout the sermon. As a result, many in the crowd sensed that this man who talked like God, somehow WAS GOD. But how could one of their own be God? It was His godlikeness that gave Jesus His tremendous authority.

SUMMARY

Throughout the sermon we've pictured Jesus standing on the side of a hill, speaking to the crowd below Him. They saw Him with their eyes and heard Him with their ears. When He finished speaking, that was the end of it. They were left with His words ringing in their heads. But that's not the end of it for us. To all born of His Spirit, He still speaks today in that "still small voice" (I Kings 19:12). It whispers INSIDE US. Though the voice is faint, it packs the SAME AUTHORITY as when Jesus spoke to the crowds that day.

Everything God does, He does BY WORDS. He has but to speak, and it's done. Whether He is saying, "LET THE DRY LAND APPEAR" . . . or, . . ."You must build your lives on My words," it is the same creative voice of the Lord. We must get used to that voice, for it is the voice of our Shepherd (John 10:4). And how do we get used to it? By spending TIME with our Lord in the Word. There is no substitute for reading God's Word and listening to the VOICE OF THE SHEPHERD. When someone asks me, "How do you know the will of God?" I reply, "Just get used to the voice of the Spirit and He will tell you what you are to do."

Please get this: the more you listen for the voice of Jesus and OBEY IT, the louder His voice sounds in your spirit. But if you ignore His voice, or resist it, the fainter it becomes. When it becomes too faint, you'll find yourself drifting further and further from the Lord and He will let you go. Then comes TROUBLE AND PAIN. It is God's way to let us learn our lessons the hard way, even to the point of going off the deep end, if necessary. He knows that in time, pain and trouble will bring us back to Him — if we're really His to begin with.

WE MUST STAY CLOSE TO THE LORD

© Linda Lovett 1974

The earliest Christians called their faith, "The Way", because it offered a WAY OF LIFE, which when followed, made them happy, successful and contented — no matter how awful their circumstances. But to continue in that life, they had to stay close to the Lord and vigorously carry out His instructions. After the first glow of salvation subsides, it's easy to neglect the Word and drift from the Lord. Like sheep, God's people tend to wander from their Shepherd. When they no longer hear His voice, they get into all sorts of trouble. Then they become fearful, troubled by hate and resentments, and all sorts of anxiety and personality distresses come upon them. Their only RELIEF is to get back to a knowledge of the Way as set forth in the sermon on the mount, and pick up on His voice again. It is His VOICE that keeps His sheep out of trouble. Should you find yourself troubled and in spiritual PAIN, return to the sermon on the mount and let the Lord put you on "The WAY" again.

SCHOOL OF KINGS

Remember how this book began? You were welcomed to the SCHOOL OF KINGS. I told you of the wonderful jobs awaiting those who applied themselves to graduate with good grades. Remember all those nice jobs? With the sermon behind you, you now know what the SCHOOL is all about. The Lord told us bluntly that we are FOOLS if we build our lives on anything but His words. This was the last thing He said. See what this means? It puts you in the SAME PLACE as those listening to Jesus that day on the mount. You, too, have to decide what you're going to do about His words.

An exciting future awaits those who take Jesus' words seriously and dare to be different. If you determine to build your life on His words, you will be different — no doubt about that. You'll find yourself sacrificing fame, family and fortune to put Him first, but you'll be glad you did, When you meet Him at heaven's gate and He says to you, "Come on in, I've been waiting for you. Wait until you see the wonderful job I have for you . . . ," it will be worth ANY SACRIFICE you've made for Him. Lest you think Jesus' standards are too high and you could never measure up, let me remind you of what you learned at the beginning . . . .

WITH GOD: TRYING IS WINNING!

FURTHER ADVENTURES WITH THE SERMON ON THE MOUNT

In the course of preparing these LIGHTS, I preached the SERMON ON THE MOUNT to my congregation and recorded it. The messages are available on 18 cassettes. That's 36 sides, 40 minutes per side. The cassettes are different from the text in your hands, for in my messages, I use illustrations and stories and make comments that cannot properly be included in a Bible commentary.

As you hear my voice from the cassette and observe how I expand the hidden meanings, it adds a new dimension to your study. Combining my voice with the LIGHTS from the text, provides a new adventure in the Sermon. In the process, you'll pick up material useful for teaching others. If you're a Sunday school teacher for example, you'll gain ideas that will make your lessons more vivid. The awesome power of THE SERMON will seize you as you behold the words on the page and listen to my voice.

For those whose eyes are dim and cannot read, the cassettes will be a blessing. But there's another way to use the cassettes that's exciting. Do you walk? Or jog? If you pick up a cassette player at a discount store, one that has a belt clip, you can take me along with you. You'll be surprised how quickly 40 minutes can go by. Not only that, you'll MASTER the Lord's sermon.

All we have today is the WORD OF GOD and the Holy Spirit. The Lord expects us to MASTER His Word, so that His Spirit can use it to CHANGE US into His likeness. The sermon on the mount is more than a sermon. It sets forth the BASICS of the Christian life. Once you master it, you won't be the same, for in the process, the SERMON will **lay hold of you**. If you like this idea, let me know, and I'll tell you how to obtain the cassettes.

C. S. Lovett

OTHER Lovett's Lights
ON THE NEW TESTAMENT YOU WILL ENJOY...

No. 538—LOVETT'S LIGHTS ON ROMANS with Rephrased Text—By C. S. Lovett ▪ 468 Lights, illustrated with drawings, graphs and paintings, 432 pages, paperback, book size 5¼" x 8¼"

No. 536—LOVETT'S LIGHTS ON ACTS with Rephrased Text—By C. S. Lovett 687 Lights, 448 pages large type, paperback, completely illustrated with drawings, paintings, graphs, and over 20 maps showing Paul's journeys, book size 5¼" x 8¼"

No. 541—LOVETT'S LIGHTS ON HEBREWS with Rephrased Text—By C. S. Lovett ▪ 279 Lights, 352 pages, paperback, illustrated with drawings, paintings, graphs, book size 5¼" x 8¼"

No. 530—LOVETT'S LIGHTS ON GALATIANS, EPHESIANS, PHILIPPIANS, COLOSSIANS, 1 & 2 THESSALONIANS with Rephrased Text—By C. S. Lovett ▪ 370 Lights, 240 pages, paperback, illustrated with drawings and maps, book size 5¼" x 8¼"

No. 526–LOVETT'S LIGHTS ON JOHN with Rephrased Text–By C.S. Lovett ▪ 588 Lights, illustrated with paintings, 336 pages, paperback, book size 5¼" x 8¼".

LOVETT'S LIGHTS BOOKLETS
(pocket-sized 3¾" x 5¾")

No. 209–LOVETT'S LIGHTS ON FIRST JOHN with Rephrased Text–By C. S. Lovett ▪ 24 pages, reduced type, 2 colors, illustrated, instruction folder.

No. 511–LOVETT'S LIGHTS ON PHILIPPIANS with Rephrased Text–By C. S. Lovett ▪ 32 pages, reduced type, 2 colors, illustrated, instruction folder.

No. 505–LOVETT'S LIGHTS ON JAMES with Rephrased Text–By C. S. Lovett ▪ 32 pages, illustrated, reduced type, 2 colors, instruction folder.

All of Dr. Lovett's works are available from:

PERSONAL CHRISTIANITY
Box 549,
Baldwin Park, California 91706

Notes:

Notes:

Notes:

Notes:

Notes: